# A BIT OF BULLTUFIS!

# A BIT OF BULLTUFIS!

Ron Montgomery

**Cover by Vi Montgomery**

**Many Hats Enterprises**
**P.O. Box 133**
**Crowsnest Pass, Alberta**
**Canada  T0K 1C0**

ISBN 0-9689800-2-3


Library and Archives Canada Cataloguing in Publication

Montgomery, Ron, 1945-
        A bit of bulltufis! / Ron Montgomery; cover, Vi Montgomery

ISBN 0-9689800-2-3
        1. Canadian wit and humour (English)  I. Title.
PS8576.O5231B58 2005 C818'.602
C2005-903439-4

# ACKNOWLEDGEMENTS

To my wife & book-partner Vi, son Cory & daughter-in-law Deana, son Perry & daughter-in-law Connie, our grand-daughter Rylee and to all our immediate and extended family members, friends and acquaintances.

Other books by Ron Montgomery:

Tales 'n Such From A Dodge City (Saskatchewan) Boomer
ISBN 0-9689800-0-7


What If Cows Yodeled?
ISBN 0-9689800-1-5

# INTRODUCTION

Humour surrounds us. The ability to look at oneself and laugh at our antics, however serious the situation may be, is a trait the author has long admired in various people. This book features another collection of short "slice-of-life" stories selected from the numerous ongoing weekly newspaper column articles written to date.

Originally from Wapella, Saskatchewan and now residing in the Crowsnest Pass, Alberta, Canada, Ron Montgomery writes full-time. These humour columns often offer a welcome outlet from the more serious side of various freelance writing assignments.

He and wife Vi (aka Dear-at-Heart) enjoy this mountainous area of Alberta, but often reflect fondly on their rural Saskatchewan upbringings. Material for these column articles comes from a number of sources both past and present.

The Writer Hard at Work

# Table of Contents

# Me, My Flubs & I

Throughout history much of mankind's destiny has been dictated by carefully thought-out planning by highly intellectual persons. Our pioneering forefathers endured incredible hardships so that we might enjoy a better life today. Others, like me for instance, have simply stumbled along life's highway relying on pure chance and the odd flub. There are positive flubs and negative flubs.

Way back when the odd fresh dinosaur egg was still showing up, I graduated from high school. Per usual, well-meaning, but misdirected people said "and what are you going to do now?" I'd pondered that question myself. One simply couldn't make slingshots and lob stones at gophers for the remainder of one's life. My parents were both quite understanding. Other kids had received stronger suggestions. Several had opened their lunch buckets to find a road map inside.

I eventually wandered off to Regina and found a part-time government job. It somehow became permanent. A positive flub. After ten years it was time for another move. Further westward. With my wife and two munchkins. After a couple of years, we eventually landed up in southern Alberta and the city of Lethbridge. This is a beautiful city and offered everything we needed for raising our family. Plus I'd somehow stumbled upon a job with a conservation organization that I'd been yearning for since leaving school. Many positive flubs.

Our kids graduated and struck out on their own. We looked at each other and said, "well now what?" Time to make another change. This time we moved smack dab into the Rocky Mountains. But still in southern Alberta. And we struck out on our own in terms of self-employment. Then the stock markets plummeted. Negative flub. Our carefully crafted plans were rapidly going up in smoke. Dear-at-Heart had landed a part-time job in our small mountain community, but a back injury forced her to leave the position. Negative flub. I was waking up bathed in sweat several nights. Explanation? At 4:00 AM the tiny connector wires in ones brain get so relaxed they become limp and short circuit. Out of proportion sweaty panic attacks are a consequence.

A few of our dear friends and relatives have recently passed on from various illnesses, diseases and just plain fluke accidents. Age is not a consideration. We'd talked with some of these same folks about their future plans. We'd shared the same uncertainties about how to maintain some semblance of balance today that might also ensure financial stability into old age. Unfortunately their carefully crafted plans now excluded one of the spouses. These were happenings with irreversible consequences. Life is ridiculously fragile.

I did a head to toe self-audit of myself the other day. Wrinkled, grey-haired, bulbous, perpetually worried, missing a tooth and prefers to subsist on foodstuffs that make dieticians develop those "no-no-please-not-that" stress-tremors. Now realize that after over a half-century on this earth, I really don't know squat about anything. But flubs obviously dictate my destiny. So

me, my flubs and I will just continue to stumble onward
hoping for the best.

A House Full of Memories

# Of Coffee & Tea

I'm a self-professed coffee junkie. And so is Dear-at-Heart. It started a few years ago when under doctor's advice I gave up imbibing on the giggle-juice. Previous to this alteration in my beverage intake the odd cup of coffee was quite suffice. And most tasted reasonably well. Or so I thought. Once coffee drinking was taken up more seriously, it became obvious that a good cup of coffee was a scarce commodity. Especially so in restaurants where coffee is normally consumed in great quantities.

Traveling about and eating in restaurants for many years through my work, I've experienced the good, the bad and the ugly when it comes to meals. What's really disappointing is enjoying a great meal, then suffering through a watered down version of what must have been intended as coffee. Or conversely you've just received a cup of coffee with supper that has obviously sat dormant on a hot plate since that morning. It's extremely hot and tastes like water from a cheap plastic canteen. Another peeve is getting a cup of coffee in an obviously un-rinsed soapy tasting cup. But there are also restaurants that serve very good coffee. These get visited often.

Buying coffee grounds or beans for your own brewing is quite an experience in itself these days. There's a whole whack of brands staring you in the face. And they all say premium. But the prices vary dramatically. Then there are the generic brands. That really throws a curve into the decision-making. It's like buying a

4

surprise grab bag from a novelty shop. Who knows what's inside the container?

Coffee machines or makers can also be a trying experience for the consumer. Some of the modern electric ones today don't look like something that would brew coffee. We have one that keeps hot water in reserve. You pour in cold water and instantly there's hot water trickling over the grounds. It's remarkably fast and if one adds the right amount of grounds it makes a superb cup of coffee. Many people, including restaurant staff, tend to be quite sparse on the amount of grounds. You end up having hot coloured water with a hint of coffee flavour.

Then there's tea. We used to drink huge amounts of tea on the farm. In fact I well-remember mom putting together a field lunch for dad and off we'd trudge. Fresh cucumber slices in homemade bread slathered with real butter. And tea served from a glass quart sealer insulated by a woolen sock or wrapped in cloth. That memory is so vivid I can almost smell the tea. And the sights, smells and sounds of a simple rural life.

My grandmother made tea in a perpetual pot that sat on a warm part of the wood-burning stove. She simply added hot water and tea leaves. Sometimes it would get quite strong and really didn't resemble tea. Another acquaintance of ours would quickly dip his tea bag into the hot water in his cup. And I mean quickly. That bag hardly had time to get thoroughly wetted down, before it was yanked out. If he was the conservative sort, one bag could conceivably last an entire month.

We also like tea. Dear-at-Heart likes both regular and herbal tea. I'm an Orange Pekoe guy. The brand doesn't really matter. If it did, I'd be in trouble. Because as with coffee there's a huge variety of teas on the shelves. Some of the non-traditional teas are very good. Some not. Like the one type we tried. It had a smoked taste. Horrible.

Years ago when hunting or cross-country skiing, I'd make tea using snow water. In an old coffee can with a wire hoop for a handle. I'd make a small fire in a cleared out area, throw some snow in the can to melt and when heated sufficiently, put in a couple of tea bags. No one shared my enthusiasm for this fine drink. To this day our two boys comment occasionally and not too kindly about my "snow-tea".

Ever notice how those little silver teapots in restaurants have a monopoly on the worst pouring spout? To begin with those little pots hold only a tiny bit more then an average cup. But when you try and pour your tea, it dribbles pitifully from the lip of the spout and down the front of the pot. So you have a napkin folded under the pot and in the saucer to sop up the tea. You can either wring the napkin out to make a full cup or ask for more hot water and repeat the process.

Well, that was quite a rant. I'm exhausted. Think I'll make a cup of tea and relax for a while. Close my eyes and be back in the field opening that quart jar and pouring the liquid into one of the old white mugs. Ah, now that's a cup of tea.

# A Windy Day Here

Southwestern Alberta is a neat area. Outdoorsy types have oodles of "things-to-do" options. The majestic Rocky Mountains are home to a wide variety of wildlife. Lakes and rivers offer superb fishing. Ditto with the foothills and prairies. Chinook winds are famous here for their ability to dramatically affect temperatures within a short time period. But those same winds can also create problems for these outdoorsy types. We consider ourselves sort of outdoorsy.

When people outside of this area mention that its windy where they live, I generally cut loose with an involuntary guffaw. (My little Webster defines guffaw as "a loud burst of laughter" so my guffaws are politically correct.) The reason for the guffaw is simply because these fine folks have no inkling of what we call "windy" here. At the time of this writing, we've had recorded gusts of up to 110 kilometres per hour. That's 68 mph. Now back to my little Webster. A hurricane is defined as "a violent storm of wind traveling over 75 mph." We're getting close. It's what we call "windy" here today.

The Crowsnest River flows nearby our house. It's a renowned fishing river and attracts people from near and far. Fly-fishing is the standard for this river, although spin casting appears to work equally as well. Now fly-fishing is an art unto itself. Simplistically a tiny synthetic tied fly is attached to a light line generally topped by a length of sinking or floating fly-line. The principle behind this method is to cast your line outward using several gentle swoops thereby eventually placing that tiny imitation "fly" smack dab in front of a hungry trout's hiding place. That's the theory.

I'm not a great fly-fisherman in calm weather conditions. The river directly behind our house has a number of trees dotting the shoreline. My gentle swoops tend to cause said fly-line to encounter said tree branches on a regular basis. Now add in some wind. Definitely not the 110 kmph stuff, but nonetheless a hefty breeze. Unless an airborne species of trout existed and lurked in tree branches, I generally go home empty-handed. Periodically a wind gust will send the fly rocketing back toward me with the sharp hook then embedded firmly in my pants or shirt. Only good fortune has saved me from a skin piercing.

We also have a couple of good fishing lakes in near proximity. But they're right in line of fire when a Chinook ensues. One does not want to be on this lake when it's windy. The frothing waves look downright unfriendly. But on a calm day this lake is a picture of tranquility and you'll be hard pressed to find a more scenic location with the surrounding tall mountains. When we lived near Lethbridge, Alberta a Chinook wind snatched our aluminum boat and sent it flying. It was impossible to hold. No damage to the boat, but the mishap did cause some sore arms.

A recent e-mail I'd sent serves as a good example of our winds: "We're blowing away here today (Saturday) --- 100 kmph winds --- Lethbridge included --- its rather wild out there. I was going to go deer or elk hunting this afternoon, but can only shoot downwind.

If I shoot westerly there's a very good chance the bullet will go out about 100 yards, lose velocity and then come tumbling back at over 100 kmph thereby possibly wounding or maiming me ---- I'm now seriously considering my options. One is to simply stay at home. Mountain living can sometimes cause paranoia."

But hey, it's not always windy here. There are also beautiful calm days. And when harsh winter weather is firmly embedded in other parts of Canada, we can enjoy some abnormally warm weather. It's a trade-off. But if you're going to complain about it being a "windy-day" in your area and that area happens to be outside southwestern Alberta, be prepared for a guffaw from me. Meanwhile I've got to check on a rumor concerning our back alley. Someone said a bighorn sheep was seen tumbling by while desperately trying to regain an upright position. That was a windy day here.

# Extremely Real Life

My little Webster defines "extreme" as the "utmost or the verge". It defines "real" as "actual, true or genuine". These are mighty popular words today. Real or reality television shows are the rage. Sports shows and the like are often called "extreme."

"Thirst" beyond needing a drink is defined as "desire vehemently". "Thrill" is to "send a quiver through". And the now totally befuddled column reader asks, exactly what are you babbling on about? Well, that we as consumers are "thirsting for thrills" and "reality" shows depicting "extreme" acts are supposedly fulfilling that need.

In my little world there's quite enough "real" stuff happens with "extreme" consequences on a daily basis. That action alone keeps my fingernails short, my hair grey, my wrinkles fresh and my lips parched.

The news networks ensure that I'm kept in a state of continuous panic. They'll throw in the odd tidbit of poignant happenings to give me a slight uplift, then immediately launch into a news piece about the oil that was used to deep-fry my potatoes. They'll then feature an expert who'll promptly expound upon the horrendous effects this oil has wreaked upon my already battered body.

Last week they'd basically toasted any hope of me living another 10 years through the astounding revelation that I'm not getting enough sleep. But just in case I decided to sleep longer, they put a cap on that too. It seems too much sleep will also toast my chances of living longer. One of our newscasts regularly throws in a brief "health" segment. Unfortunately any credibility I'd first given these pieces is completely shot. It's like dry comedy.

Our stock market situation today offers realism at its finest. If our situation is relatively representative, then there doesn't appear to be a single person in the investment world that has one iota of knowledge on what's going on. But they're all self-proclaimed experts. It drives me nuts.

The gurus talk as if it was their money and future at risk. Heck they're still making money on a salary while telling us how much we've lost. But not to worry since the markets will come back. Unfortunately barring a miracle, the "projected" monies we've lost to date just plain won't be back in our usable lifetime. That's real. But not to worry, say the gurus. And they're probably right. I'll either oversleep or eat one too many french-fry.

Our Jeep developed a rattling sound in the exhaust system. It was just before Christmas. Drat, said I. Probably a muffler and probably expensive. Bravely trundling off to the muffler shop, the folks there happily put "rattle" on the hoist and offered their prognosis. It's your catalytic converter and your muffler also has a small leak. Okay, said I --- and how much will that cost? Oh that'll be a little over seven hundred dollars. A herd of two thousand quivers stampeded through my body. I was "thrilled" ---- extremely.

Trying to stay calm, I swallowed several times, then located enough mouth moisture to squeakily request that they just remove the converter and put in a straight pipe. That way Dear-at-Heart will still possibly get a Christmas present from me. Nay, said the trusty hoping-to-be-rich muffler tech --- no can do. Engine computer will get severely ticked off and throw everything out of whack. You see those little wires? They're sensors. You need a catalytic converter. What I really needed was a strong headache pill. That confounded blankity-blank engine computer was obviously in cahoots with these diamond-studded catalytic converters. This was surreal. And Webster says --- (oh, knock it off already and just use a different word.)

But hey, I've been lured into watching some of that "real" televised stuff too. It's entertainment and we're all "thirsty". Incidentally my catalytic converter continues to rattle. And I sincerely hope that engine computer is still ticked off. That makes two of us. And that's real life - extremely.

# The Handy-Man

Marriage is a traumatic event for most men. You've just agreed to share the rest of your life with someone else. And like the vows say, that includes for better or worse. But it doesn't stop there. This likely includes helping to raise a small herd of munchkins. Plus you're now officially committed to trying to repair things.

And also helping your significant other with tasks that she might from time to time let you do. Such as helping out in the kitchen. Once you've successfully passed your probationary period, you may even be allowed periodic times of reasonably free rein in the kitchen. Depending of course on who might be coming over to dinner.

You'll sometimes notice ads in the newspaper offering "handyman" services. This is not to be confused with the married definition. Even the spelling is different. The married version is called a "handy-man" --- two distinct words. He's handy and is obviously a man. My little Webster defines "handy" in a few ways including "convenient for use". That appears to best fit the married version. In my case, unfortunately I'm also somewhat "handy-man" challenged in certain tasks.

Dear-at-Heart has completely given up on me making the first cut of a large onion. Inevitably I'm accused of cutting the wrong end and therefore potentially bringing plagues of onion distress raining down upon us. Or causing the onion to collapse prematurely, which it actually does seem to do. I however did not know there was a wrong end to an onion and apparently still don't realize that fact. There's still some hope, however slight that may be. We've only been married 36 years. The probationary period for those males who find wedded bliss in south-eastern Saskatchewan is apparently 40 years. I've got 4 years to sort out this blight in my onion-judgment.

When "things" break around the house, you are most definitely the official "handy-man". Expectations may run high. The "handy-man" designation is likely also responsible for the fact I've accumulated approximately 78 screwdrivers (there may actually be 79, hence the word approximate). There's also a mammoth supply of various types of strings, glues, sealants, nails, screws and so on in stock. It's quite overwhelming and also somewhat embarrassing. I have so many knick-knacks that many times when in need of a certain item I'll have to run out and buy it. It's there in the garage, somewhere, but I have no idea where.

Fixing leaky faucets is a "handy-man" specialty. But the people that make these faucets are quite aware that any red-blooded handy-man will consider himself a plumber of great renown. So the faucet people will seldom make any two taps alike. Even the same brands are apt to require different size washers. I have containers full of faucet washers and springs. But whenever I'm in need of one, none of the ones in my stock will ever fit. So I buy another pack and throw the extras into one of my containers. It's a vicious circle.

A real "handy-man" is also an electrician of questionable renown. The people that made those electric kettles a few years ago must have strived to ensure the connections inside the plate under the kettle would self-destruct after a certain period of time. They likely thought people would simply buy a new kettle. But they forgot to factor in the "handy-man". I've fixed many of those kettles over the years. Some of them several times over.

Dryers, stoves, washing machines and dishwashers will all develop an electrical problem at some point. The "handy-man" will try to fix this. Sometimes he'll accidentally succeed. And then expect accolades from his adoring family. But in many cases his efforts will only succeed in giving him an electrical problem too. He'll labour over the problem for several hours, skin his knuckles, utter words that have absolutely no meaning in this galaxy and eventually blow his own internal fuse. Then call an electrician or plumber. Long-live the "handy-man".

# The Adult Living Quandary

As if more confirmation were needed to confirm that I'm getting older, great gobs of flyers and magazines laden with adult living ads arrive in our mail almost daily. This glitzy promotion of the increasingly popular "adult-living" lifestyle is reaching near epidemic distribution. Seen through my frugally conscious eyes, this can be one danged expensive option to basically avoid mingling with young children and slobbering dogs. But I'm likely missing the point.

We lease a campsite on a nearby lake where our trailer sits year round. There was a choice of sites. The owner casually glanced at my grey hair, wrinkled face, missing tooth and slightly bulbous figure. He kindly advised us that, "one section of the campsite was primarily occupied by folks around our age". It was quieter, he said. "We'll take it", said we.

He was partially right. Some of the "old-folks" still like to whoop it up on occasion. But unless their older children use their site while unsupervised, the whoops are generally pretty feeble. The resident wildlife is even convinced that this area is off limits for all but the older critters. We have geriatric coyotes in this particular area. They'll cut loose with a series of yodels until about 11:00 PM, which soon dies down to pitiful little yips eventually followed by complete silence. The effort must leave these old coyotes plumb exhausted.

In various cities, we've seen the outer walls of a number of adult living communities. The walls look pretty nice. Many of these wall-tops are rounded. It must be a throwback to days of yore, when invading armies would use grappling hooks to scale the castle walls. If that ancient design thwarted invading armies, then these modern walls also make sense. Thwarting invading hordes of rowdy youngsters who might resort to access by grappling hook is a thought. A moat with an operable drawbridge would thwart both unwanted youngsters and slobbering dogs.

The ads for these adult living communities are hard on my self-esteem. The people always look so incredibly fit and well groomed. The men have smooth, tanned faces and are usually carrying a jacket or light sweater thrown casually over a shoulder. The ladies have remarkably clear complexions and are generally shown gazing serenely, either upon the impeccable, gorgeous, groomed landscape or their impeccable, gorgeous, groomed mate.

This befuddles me. My perpetually worried face will always look like an eroded anthill following a major rainfall. The wrinkles are deep and sinuous. Each line has a story. My glasses cover up the baggy eyes. Inactivity and a love of food have left me with a rather strange looking figure. My chest took to roaming over the years. It's finally found a preferred perch just above my beltline.

I like those practical flannel lined shirt-jackets. They're comfy. Here in southern Alberta you don't throw a jacket over your shoulder. It would up and blow away. And be immediately set upon by a herd of unruly youngsters and slobbering dogs. And maybe that's the point of adult living communities.

Our Leased Site at Lake Koocanusa

# Excuses Galore

"Dad-gum-it anyway, this stupid gun couldn't hit the broad side of a barn door at 10 paces", says the blossoming, but slightly misled Daniel-Boone wannabe after a clean miss with his 12 gauge double on a tight flock of 50 hovering mallard ducks at the dazzling distance of 50 feet. He holds the gun out parallel to his body and gives it a sizzling look, whilst turning it slowly about obviously looking for the flaw that caused this embarrassing miss. It certainly wasn't his fault. No way, it was that stupid, blankety-blank gun. Given a little time, we can darn near come up with an excuse for anything. Some of us are very good at it.

Fishermen have been the brunt of many a joke when it comes to excuses and downright fibs. Perhaps some of it is deserving; some is plain myth. It's a fairly easy sport to levy blame on a whole host of things, besides your poor fishing skills. The weather, improper fishing gear, dull hooks, wrong bait, wrong time of month, wrong depth, there's no fish in this area and so on. A small credibility problem arises when one says the uncaught fish saw his reflection in the water, smelled the onion on his breath, sensed that he really didn't want to clean fish that day or didn't like the colour of his boat. One of those handy, dandy fish finders has pros and cons. It shows fish are present which is helpful, it also shows that you can't catch squat. The instruction booklet should include a section dedicated to excuses.

When one has never normally had a weight problem, but suddenly seems to have swallowed a bloat-button, a rapid search and blame ensues. "My thingamajig in control of fat disposal is kaput. Might have to see the doctor. Same thing happened back in grade four. Blossomed out like one of them there helium balloons. Ate lots of rhubarb and my thingamajig got better all on it's own. Can't eat rhubarb now. Fish don't like the smell."

Even bodily damage is blamed on something other then plain clumsiness. Hitting a finger with the hammer is a biggie. "Great gobs of magnificent ouches, that stupid, blasted hammer" and at this point it gets thrown over your shoulder and you're sucking on the wounded finger while prancing about also doing a slow motion pivot. Meanwhile the disgraced hammer has just squarely done a head-conk on Rover, who was lying patiently nearby waiting for you to hit your finger and entertain him once more.

Locking ones keys in the car is the supreme act of automobile embarrassment. If it happens in a fairly busy place it again has pros and cons. On the downside you're convinced everyone thinks you're a forgetful klutz. You are. On the upside someone will come to try and open your car. Meanwhile as they're busy helping, you're babbling on about how those keys got locked in the car in the first place. "That goofy wind did that to me once before. Just stepped out of the car and poof come a blast of wind. Knocked me flat, keys flew out my hand, somehow landed back in the ignition and whack, the danged door slammed shut. Wouldn't you know it?"

Everyone gets lost in strange city at one time or another. It keeps life exciting and tests your marriage vows. You know, the one that says "for better or worse". If you both get too frazzled the "sickness and health" vow might eventually become an issue. Anyway you've gotten severely lost. And it was the signs fault. The goofy things are always in the wrong place even when they're in the right place. "Well, of all the stupid places to put a sign. How the heck was I supposed to know that was my turn? And the paints faded. Thought it said Mapella, not Wapella. Now it looks like this sign says we're on our way to Goosomin. Where the heck's that? Wonder if there's any fishing there?"

Enjoying the Day

# Pass the Potatoes

There's quite a number of food shows on television these days. And they feature a large cross-section of offerings to please virtually every palate. I enjoy these shows. The chefs are for the most part quite entertaining. Audience members can be hilarious too. Surely some of these responses are staged. Many audience members are practically salivating. Me too, but at least I'm at home.

It's ironic that on one hand we have supposed concerns over weight problems affecting all ages of society today. Then we have food shows showing these talented chefs cooking scrumptious looking offerings that likely use "no-no" base ingredients similar to what our mothers and grandmothers used. Heavy cream, real butter and so on. But that's likely why it's so enjoyable for me to watch. Plus most of the chefs readily admit the influence of their mother's cooking.

Now granted many of the gourmet dishes are true works of art and probably not applicable to mealtimes in most Canadian homes. But gosh, some of those desserts and even the main courses look unbelievably delicious. We once had occasion to enjoy some of those gourmet meals and other specialties while in the Maritimes. The conference we attended included outings to a variety of high-end hotels and restaurants. Plus a cooking school and a special evening, where the best of PEI was featured. Wow, it was truly food bliss.

Unfortunately all these niceties aside, I couldn't help but think of the threshing crews that used to visit our farm. Or the wood-sawing crew. These guys never ate. They simply inhaled food in massive quantities. Presentation was not a concern. Just pass the potatoes and bring on the pie. Dainty drizzles of honey or caramel over a tiny scoop of carefully prepared cheesy dessert topped off with an edible flower would only create havoc. Likely as not they'd wonder why in the world each of them now had a boutonniere. Where we threshing or going to a wedding?

Same thing with mom and her cooking efforts. There were six munchkins in her crew. Just ensuring no one ate the tablecloth by mistake was a challenge. Dear-at-Heart's mother had nine girls to contend with in her family. Now that's downright intimidating for a number of reasons. And forget about the myth that girls eat less then boys. Until the age of eighteen or thereabouts, both boys and girls require massive amounts of fuel in the form of foodstuffs. Lethargic children could not effectively harass harried parents.

Bread baking in our house was done a scale normally reserved for factory production. Cookie baking was an exercise in futility. We ate them quicker then mom could cook them. Same thing with regular meals. Reflecting back on those times creates nostalgia mixed with angst. For now I feel guilty. But also very impressed that our mothers and grandmothers could cope with feeding such large families without any of the conveniences we now take for granted.

Even today it's a wonder to me how long it takes to prepare a meal and then how quickly it's all over with. You can spend hours putting together various dishes lovingly prepared and carefully thought out. Then with a mighty whoosh, two belches and a yawn, that big special occasion supper is kaput. Now you're left looking at a mammoth heap of incredibly yucky pots, pans and dishes. If you're fortunate most will go into a dishwasher. If not, then someone is going to have some mighty wrinkled, pathetic looking dishwater-hands.

So does this gourmet food prepared by talented chefs have its place? You bet it does. Most of those exquisite looking dishes are not only prepared in a manner to tease the visual senses, they also taste incredibly good. I'm hooked on a lot of those dishes. Unfortunately in many cases the cost of enjoying these chef-prepared offerings is out of reach. But that's okay; I'm quite flexible when it comes to food. Just pass the potatoes and bring on the pie.

# Downright Thrilling

My brother was strolling through the kitchen, when his sister innocently said something like "Hi Ralph". He gave a startled jump and for all intents was momentarily scared out of his wits. Sis was not hiding and leaping out to say "boo" but the result was the same. This has probably happened to all of us at some point and like that ad states invariably we get the "oh-what-a-thrill" feeling.

I'd been checking on some vacant properties for the purposes of meeting insurance requirements on behalf of a firm that had them up for sale. One of those homes always gave me the willies. There were two years of these weekly checks. My hair would just get relaxed so it could be combed flat again and it would be time for another weekly check. Why this happened, I have no idea. But my inner sense was obviously not happy about something in that house. Departure was always joyous.

An animal scare also manages to send my hair into electric spasms and multitudes of those mysterious "goose bumps" magically appear on my arms. The after effect can be rather chilling as you can almost feel your entire body rippling in relief. Maybe you're meandering along and a large dog lunges out behind a hedge barking furiously and threatening to eat you. If you're lucky enough to escape unscathed, it seems like a couple of weeks have passed before all your goose bumps recede.

As mentioned before, heights are also a problem for me. Not while in helicopters or small planes. But put me on a carnival ride and anything beyond the merry-go-round is downright scary. Ferris-wheels are out of the question. The last one I went on was many years ago and I'm not sure my body has ever fully recovered. If the view was spectacular, I wasn't aware of this fact. My eyes were scrunched shut and my teeth were clenched. On the downturns my upper lip covered my nose and I couldn't breathe properly. Departure was exceedingly joyous that time.

Then there are the ghost stories. Now I don't know about you, but under the right circumstances and depending on the storyteller, these tales can and do provide a level of major mind-disturbance. If the person telling the story is quite credible, I'm in probable believer-mode. If the storyteller is an older person and not excessively under the influence of Uncle Yaks melt-the-paint homebrew then I'm a goner in terms of bodily responsive ghost-thrills. And there are plenty of those ghost stories.

We'd attended a writer's conference in the Maritimes and I had the good fortune of sharing the same tour van with a lady author who had written several books on Maritime ghosts. Her research was based on actual interviews and in many cases included a tour of the supposedly haunted house. She was an older lady and therefore instantly won my respect for the credibility of the tales. And she was remarkably confident, which gave me the jitters. She'd not only felt the presence of these ghosts in others homes, but had a couple of friendly ones in her residence.

For me this was like nothing I've ever experienced. The more she talked, the more spooked I became. The more spooked I became, the more questions I asked. It was the ultimate thrill. I was on a ghost "high". Thank goodness we'd done the sightseeing tour in broad daylight and in the company of other writers. As it was, my arms sported marble-sized goose bumps that were hanging by threads. Several fell off. They could have been used as slingshot ammo.

Thrill seekers are everywhere. They go out of their way to scare the daylights out of their own bodies. Television shows that share these thrill seekers stunts with viewers are in an out war for popularity. To appease thrill seekers seated in their armchairs. We humans are indeed a funny bunch. Most of us are rather timid souls quite content to just enjoy the ride through life's experiences with the odd thrill. But for others the entire ride needs to be downright thrilling.

# Making Our Own Bologna Sandwich

"Yuk, this is terrible", said the worker in disgust after his first bite. His co-worker asked him why he didn't order a different take-out sandwich if he didn't like bologna. "Oh, I make my own sandwiches", said the worker. (Just for the record, I for one really enjoy a bologna & mustard sandwich.)

But this true story serves to illustrate an important point in our everyday lives. In one way or another we too make our own bologna sandwiches. Then writhe in discomfort over the consequences.

Someone said the hardest word many can say is "no". So when asked to participate in something we truly dislike, we're instead apt to agree to do it. Perhaps it involves fundraising. You're supposed to solicit businesses and individuals. You don't like solicitors. Your house even has a sign that says, "no soliciting". This bologna sandwich is going to be understandably hard to chew. But hey, you made the darn thing, so munch away and cut the complaining.

Most men hate to ask for help. They're fixers. So when the car breaks down, it's imperative that we men have to see if we can repair it. After ample mutterings have turned the air blue, fingers are suitably skinned and the car engine still sounds like a herd of hungry pigs at feeding time, it's bona fide mechanic time. This is one bologna sandwich that's truly difficult to swallow.

Family gatherings can be great fun. But someone has to feed the gang. Inevitably there'll be someone who offers to provide the whole kit and caboodle. The "nahlet's-potluck-it" suggestion is shushed into oblivion. The big day arrives and the food hostess is a wreck. Not only for that day but also for the entire following week. A whole tray of bologna sandwiches for this self-inflicted gesture.

As one ages, your body is no longer quite up to snuff. It now aches over seemingly minor exertions. But that portion of your mind in charge of muscle patrol is stuck in a time warp. It thinks you're still twenty-one. And even though you can now afford to hire a bit of help, you're still pretty darned tight. So you decide to re-shingle the roof yourself. It's a high roof and it's a windy time of year. Enjoy - you've just made yourself a six-layered bologna sandwich.

Many people today appear to be obsessed with seeing how many "toys" they can accumulate. A boat, quads, dirt bikes, snowmobiles, flat deck trailer, huge camping trailer and so on adorn the driveways of many homes. A big gas-guzzling truck is needed to pull the trailer. And one needs to work quite hard in order to make all the payments on this conglomeration. Time-off is a rarity. The boat got used once last year, the quads twice and the big camper four times. This is a popular bologna sandwich.

Well, must go. Promised to give a talk at the school. Kind of nervous, but maybe a bologna sandwich will settle me down.

Enjoying Our Beautiful Mountain Landscape

# Our Horse Eats Gas

Most horses eat grass and emit gas. Ours eats gas and tries to avoid grass. Now look me straight in the paragraph and tell me that isn't confusing? Well its actually quite explainable. Our horse is called Honda. It's a 1990 Honda 300 4WD ATV otherwise known simply as a quad. It eats gas, not grass. And not wanting to severely damage our outdoor environment, Honda and I try mightily to stick to established trails and avoid grass.

We used to have horses on the farm. Some were workhorses meant to pull various as a team and a couple were for riding. But that was so long ago I'd all but forgotten the tumbles. Until Honda also sent us for a tumble, which was not only undignified, but also tough on half-century old and already well abused, shins and elbows. Honda's brief attempt at a wild runaway immediately ended when a tree on the steep down slope refused to be bowled over.

After leaving the farm and moving to a number of locations in pursuit of all-important work, we eventually landed up in south-western Alberta. This is cowboy country. As a youngster I used to live and breathe cowboy stuff. Given the fact most grown-ups are just youngsters with more experience, I'd yearned for a horse through all these working years. Alas that just wasn't practical.

Then we moved to the mountains. But still in town, so no acreage or place to keep a horse. Charging up mountain trails using footsmobile was out of the question. My get up and go had gotten lost several years ago. I believe it was accidentally left behind in a booth at a fast food restaurant in Lethbridge roughly ten years ago. In any case there were mountains beckoning and my wheezy body needed a solution. Time was marching onward. My eyesight might be next on the kaput-list.

Aha - how about a quad? It could be our substitute horse. What a stupendously brilliantly deduced idea. Upside. No barn required. No horse pucks, as cleanup after a quad would be minimal. Food storage would be a breeze. A few containers of gas and that was it. Outside of insurance and a license plate plus a bit of periodic maintenance, overall costs would be relatively manageable. Downside. Quads aren't warm and don't respond to talk. I wasn't familiar with riding a quad. Very few quads if any have been known to "whinny". You don't sit as high on a quad as on a horse. But neither do you have as far to fall. You might look silly wearing a cowboy hat and cowboy boots while riding a quad. But that silly thing really doesn't seem to be a factor anywhere in life today. Hmmm - yep, a quad could pretty much be justified.

So we bought our quad. The first few times while both loading and unloading off the utility trailer using those steel ramps was a tad awkward. While loading the quad at the dealership, I gave it too much gas, shot up the ramps and darned near impaled myself on the front wall of the trailer. Unloading was similar. The quad came flying down the ramps at warp speed and I just hung on for dear life hoping it would stay in a straight line. Eventually the highly sensitive gas lever was sorted out.

Our first excursion was up a fairly steep trail in the nearby mountains. Dear-at-Heart was perched behind me as I gingerly coaxed Honda up the trail trying to sort out the right gears. This wasn't as easy as it looked when I'd seen others go shooting past. Downshifting while going up a slope caused the quad's front to lift slightly. Much like a horse rearing up. Once in awhile I'd downshift too far and hit neutral. Then we'd be rolling backward on the slope. This caused angst, which in turn activated my sweat glands. Excess angst also causes me to mutter. As I muttered, it caused Dear-at-Heart to strengthen her death grip on the excess flesh covering my ribs. I don't blame her for seeking a handhold in the least. And it was reassuring to know those two prominent bodily side-handles were good for something.

Going back down the steep trail was also tricky. The front brakes had more "oomph" then the back ones. Gravity crushed both of us to the front and the quad threatened to topple forward every time I'd "oomph" on the front brakes too much. A combination of "whoops-oomph" and a large loose rock caused Honda to topple sideways. Both of us novice riders were dumped unceremoniously in a heap on the trail. Our gas-guzzling horse called Honda had just bucked us off. This substitute horse thing was obviously working out well.

# Tender Tootsies Get No Respect

One would think that the big toes are the toughest of all five on each foot. Mine aren't. Their role is like that of a bodyguard. They take the brunt of all hits intended for little toes and far from being a toughie instead cause no end of whining from my brain cells in charge of pain alert. If it's a really big hit, my toe will throb in seemingly direct harmony with my heartbeat. Holding the wounded toe and rocking back and forth is somewhat soothing, but only temporary at best. Putting on a sock followed by a shoe, then trying to walk is a delicate matter.

I'm always amazed how durable some people's feet appear to be. When much younger, I'd traipse about barefoot quite a bit. And outside of stepping on a sharp object, blunt protrusions like small rocks and so on never really hurt. Now if I shed my socks and shoes and attempt to walk across gravel, I'm taking those huge dainty steps normally associated with Great Blue Herons. Attempting to cross a paved road while barefoot is another sight to behold. Many people look like they're adopting a karate stance with both arms hung straight out like featherless wings and gingerly crossing the road on tiptoes with those same huge dainty steps.

Cast iron griddles are heavy. Especially when after a 3-foot long free fall, they land on a big toe. That happened over four months ago and my toenail still sports the mark. What's intriguing is noting how much ones toenails must grow. Mine must grow quite slowly. The mark has moved from the original place at the base of the nail to only the halfway point. Maybe like the rest of me any upward growth is now stunted. By default after age 50 all growth is outward in favour of providing an ample cushioning effect in the event of possible tumbles. (I think there was a scientific study completed somewhere supporting this notion.)

Clipping ones toenails is a necessary task, but can be difficult depending upon stature. If one were so inclined one could possibly have others clip your toenails. But normally this is a self-administered venture. Being rather brittle by nature, flying toenail fragments can be disbursed anywhere within a 10-foot radius of the cutter's point of origin. Ricochets can propel these fragments even further.

Toenail cutting is a delicate matter. If one uses scissors and one has poor eyesight, you're quite apt to slice off a goodly portion of skin along with your piece of toenail. Using those specially designed toenail clippers is fine, but one can easily cut off too much toenail. Then you're left with a tender hunk of totally unprotected toe. If this happens, it's amazing how that area even feels vulnerable. Guess your toenails are there for a good reason.

My feet don't get much respect. They're constantly being abused. If it's really cold outside, my feet are likely cold. If my shoes get wet, my feet get wet. If my feet get tired, but I'm not yet at my destination, they have to just trudge onward. The rest of my body is really just along for the ride. If I overeat, my feet still have to support the extra weight. Much like a designated driver, they're ultimately responsible for getting me home.

Yep, I'd better start giving these feet a little more respect. They've actually got a lot of responsibility. The next time my sock slips down and bunches up under my foot, I'll have to stop and clear the wrinkle right away. And maybe even ask my feet if they're ready to go yet the next time we're out at a buffet. Got to look after these tender tootsies.

# One Confused Fish 'Er Man?

The old fishing net that either trailed behind a rowboat or was thrown into a river worked great for catching relatively large quantities of fish. Barbed spears or small barbed bone hooks were also used to catch a meal or two. Our ancestors would be astounded to see us fishermen of today.

No longer content to simply catch and eat fish, we now prefer to play with them. In fact many people that pursue their fish of choice never even eat them. Phew - -are you joking? No siree, give me a good slab of beef any day. But man alive, do I ever like catching them. And catch them, they do. To the extent that in many areas those creative barbs from our ancestors days are no longer allowed. That's right. Kaput!

The people that mostly don't eat fish anyway, but love to play with them have obviously caught the attention of the armchair bound fish-rulers. A scenario. "Hmmm", said the fish-rulers, "how can we show the boys with the bucks that we're really looking after their play toys. Hey, how bout we make everybody get rid of those goofy barbs. In fact, whose bright idea was it to put barbs on hooks anyway? Look at how long a de-clawed cat could play with a live mouse. Same mouse could entertain twenty de-clawed cats. Long as they don't handle the critter too roughly. Might work, might not, but its worth a shot and besides who'll ever question us anyway? We're the experts."

Fishing regulations today are a tad confusing too. Certain areas allow so many fish of said species, so long as its such and such size. If you happen to catch so many of such and such size, then you're only allowed one more of such and such size. But on such and such stretch of river you can't keep any fish until such and such date. However the good news is you can use such and such bait beginning at such and such date. But mind you it's only from this such and such landmark to that such and such landmark on such and such river. With bait defined as such and such. And remember now no barbed hooks. "Whaddya mean its canned salmon time? Hey you forgot to buy your license?"

On the brighter side, some things in the world of fishing haven't changed dramatically. Diehard fishermen still eventually develop really long arms. Much like the giraffe and its long neck, this is an evolutionary miracle born of necessity. With his long neck, the giraffe can reach otherwise unattainable succulent leaves high up in the tree branches. With his widespread arms, an avid fisherman can describe the prize that narrowly escaped his incredibly talented attempts to garner the big one. Short arms simply wouldn't do the escapee justice.

Yep, it's really unfortunate that CS (aka common sense) disease has so adversely afflicted our society today. Fishing can be fun. And surprisingly enough, most fish are still edible. But hey, all barbs aside, happy fishing!

A Hardy Fisherman

# The Campfire Blues

You could see the smoke from several kilometers away. It looked like the beginnings of a forest fire. Except the smoke was wispy and scattered. Entering the park it became quite evident where this was originating. It was evening and since all campers like to be viewed as die-hard outdoorsy types, most campsites had a fire going. Getting that fire going could be highly entertaining. If you were a bystander.

Frontier books and movies usually portray the lighting of a fire as a simple task. It always did and actually still does amaze me how the hero would either quickly beach his canoe, swing down from his horse or pause his fleeing on foot from hostile forces to quickly light a fire and boil up a pot of coffee. Plus fry up a pan of sliced slab bacon. And it all happened in less then one paragraph or a one-minute movie clip.

There wasn't any newspaper handy to be crushed up, nor a fire-starting block from one of the sporting goods stores on hand. No siree, these guys would throw together a few twigs, strike a lucifer (my cowboy heroes often times called their matches lucifers) and poof, before you could say "phew, was that me or the horse" they'd be squatted on their haunches drinking coffee, eating bacon and wiping the bacon drippings from the pan with a hefty slab of sourdough bread.

These hardy souls generally ate a pound of bacon in one squat and drank down several cups of coffee. That was it. No veggies for them. Then they'd casually light up a roll-your-own smoke. Maybe the tobacco leaves counted as a veggie substitute to fulfill part of the recommended frontier daily food group intake.

Their fire was generally always tiny so there'd be a minimum amount of smoke. That way their pursuers or any other badniks in the vicinity wouldn't see any campfire smoke. Astounding foresight. Assuming my fire even eventually lights, there's usually an abundance of smoke being spewed. Any wildlife in the immediate vicinity instinctively flees fearing the worst.

Lighting fires with twigs is now mostly an urban myth. At approximately $5.00 or more per bundle for firewood in many formal campsites nowadays, you'd possibly be lynched for stealing twigs. As a result, these sticks of firewood become precious and hold distinct monetary value. Lighting one's fire can thus be a stressful procedural nightmare.

A few slices of kindling garnered from the firewood and placed over a tiny wad of scrunched up newspaper is a futile effort. Ten minutes later, this lighting effort is probably repeated. Fifteen minutes later the entire remaining newspaper is scrunched beneath a most impressive teepee of wood. It stays lit. But your so-called friendly campfire now resembles a morbid funeral pyre. And you're nearly out of wood. Squatting cramps your legs. Assuming you can actually hold a squat without keeling over into a wobbly heap. And the billowing smoke follows you all around the fire pit. Oh well, your doctor is likely opposed to you consuming bread-sopped bacon grease anyway.

By Golly, It's Actually Producing a Flame

# Pot Bellied Labs

We'd recently looked after our son's young Labrador Retriever dog for a month while the family was on holidays. Indy is a good little dog, but full of energy. A little over a year-old, she needs both attention and exercise. Up until a few years ago when our own aging dog passed on, we've always had dogs in our life. But as Delta became older, so did we. It was a good match.

Short of getting an older dog from the humane society, which is quite fine too, I'm wondering; is there a need to produce young dogs with old dog characteristics for the geriatric crowd? One does get attached to their dogs, so this would still allow a relatively long approximate ten-year relationship to take place.

Old dogs and older people generally like to relax in the evening. Young dogs have no yearning to relax and are constantly seeking attention. If you scratch your old dogs ears once between 7 PM and the National news, he's good for the whole evening. And so are you.

Old dogs mostly like to snack, not binge on a huge meal. That works out well too. When you have 9 PM cheese and crackers, Rover gets a milk bone. You can sigh in unison at the combined exertion, then once more contentedly stretch out on your favourite respective lounging sites. And patiently await the National.

Old dogs tend to arise slowly and gingerly work out their stiffness before tottering off to wherever you're heading. Older people generally arise in the same manner. A young dog simply launches itself off to nowhere in particular. Leaving you to figure out both where it went and why.

A young dog that had to walk at a slow pace would be a big plus. You often see red-faced puffing people with long sinuous spaghetti-like arms being dragged along behind their beloved fast-pacing pooch. In most cases and if one were remotely truthful the dog is actually taking the owner for a walk.

And old dogs like to poke along sniffing at everything, but mostly quite content to be within two steps of your foot. A walk is quite pleasant. Young dogs are full of curiosity and are quite certain the items of most interest are either over the next hill or around the next bend. Both you and the old dog have darn near seen it all, which is good since neither of you any longer possess keen eyesight.

Old dogs generally have lumps, bumps and potbellies with prominent ribs. Plus grey whiskers and runny eyes. You and your old dog look compatible. Otherwise it's like seeing an older gentlemen strolling along with a young lass on his arm that is most certainly not his adoring granddaughter. Although the old gentlemen's buddies may initially feel a twinge of envy, they actually feel sorry for him. For they just saw Ernie the ancient shoot by behind a young spaniel. Instead of sauntering along with a potbellied Lab.

An Old Friend

# I'm Not a Golfer

Golf. This is one game that has me totally mystified. The mystification comes from several factors. It's hugely popular. One person can play if one chooses to do so. It can be a social outing. It can be a business outing. It can provide some exercise in the form of walking. But like the saying goes, and cutting through all of the above, you're basically just hitting this little ball and then pursuing it up and down man-made hills, possibly through sand and possibly even in water. You spend your entire life raising children, pursuing them up and down and through everything. You're stressed. Now you play golf. And it's relaxing?

I'm a "gee-do-I-have-to" golfer. The odd time someone drags me kicking and screaming into a game, it's left me feeling very klutzy. I know zip about the game, other then one is trying desperately to get that tiny pockmarked ball from this spot over to and into that little hole. And the only way to accomplish this with any amount of success is to severely whack the ball with a hefty golf club in the general direction of that little hole. The less whacks, the better.

Not being satisfied with being able to wield only one club, there's a whole myriad of these clubs to choose from. Apparently there's a club for every possible situation thereby eliminating any chance of fabricating an excuse as to why you performed poorly. These clubs are apparently not cheap. And neither is the case. Or the little cart to pull these clubs and its case about.

Being a rather cautious sort my initial concern was not to hit one of those people off to the side of my line of fire. But there were also people coming up behind me waiting to use my launching pad. I was beginning to feel a tad stressed. The first mighty swing was akin to shooting a black powder rifle when everything beyond the barrel is a haze of smoke. In my case it was a bombardment of shredded turf. And a lot of it. There was no way to separate the ball out of all that flying grass and disintegrating dirt. Thankfully one of my buddies said a fellow about a hundred feet to my left had stopped it with his shin. My neck was starting to ache.

Some people were scooting about in a golf cart. They looked like they could benefit from a good walk. But they were a happy lot and were swigging back the giggle-juice with great gusto. In fact this entire scenario looked quite like a high society social outing. Huddles of well-dressed tanned folks with special shoes, gloves and chipper looking hats. Then one of those dapper gentlemen missed getting the pockmarked ball into the little hole from a rather close distance. That's when I noticed the striking similarity between colourful golf-language and that used by some patrons that frequent seedy city bars. "Gosh" was not included.

One does see some fantastic golf courses in any travels. And they're not limited only to the cities or larger centers. Many smaller communities have very nice settings and are generally quite affordable relative to the larger centers. Even if one isn't a golfer, one has to appreciate the grounds keeping that go into these courses. They're picture-perfect.

So where and when did this game of golf start? My reference goes way back to the Middle Ages, but apparently the modern game of golf as we know it originates from Scotland and was well established by 1457. It's thought the first golf balls were made of wood, succeeded by balls filled with compressed, boiled feathers in the early 17$^{th}$ century. The rubber-cored ball made its debut in 1898. The term "caddie" apparently comes from the Old French "cadet".

So there you have it. I don't currently play golf, but might some day. One just never knows. So hats off to all the participants in this game called golf. Meanwhile, if you ever are on a golf course and see what appears to be a badger digging with great gusto in pursuit of a gopher, look again. Those flying clods of dirt could be caused by my frantic slashes at that little ball just trying to get it airborne. Where it's heading is a low priority. You'd be wise to keep a sharp eye out for an incoming ball, even if you're in the lounge. I'm not a golfer. "Fore."

# Behind Closed Doors

Remember that hit song from years past titled "Behind Closed Doors"? In a nutshell, I like to think it says we never really know what goes on behind any closed doors, be it a home, apartment, camper or for that matter even a vehicle. That was a neat song theme and it brings to mind all sorts of images. Just think about your own lives and what little privacy we would have if we never had doors to close - interesting isn't it?

When one got married the vows likely included "for better or worse". I wonder if it included watching Mr. Scruff groggily wandering about in their Fruit of the Loom, unshaven, smacking his lips in the futile hopes of getting rid of that horrid morning breath, whilst struggling to get the Nabob into the right part of the new coffee machine? Or seeing Mrs. Oh-So-Pretty with a head chock full of those mammoth hair curlers that bear a remarkable resemblance to small rolls of fence wire possibly re-designed to confine midget chickens?

What about eating at home versus eating at a restaurant? Do you conduct yourself the same? Or wear appropriate clothing with a well-groomed appearance? Some might, but somehow I suspect the majority likes to "relax". Others may just kick back and noisily chow down on whatever suits their fancy, happily belching, smacking and wiping away to their heart's content. Especially if it's a feed of honey-garlic drippy chicken wings or heaps of large sauce-slathered beef ribs. Break out the napkins.

Television watching is relaxation at its finest. Or at least it should be. But an ultra-spooky horror movie or a highly competitive sports game can bring forth all sorts of reactions from people. One of our past acquaintances used to be a wrestling fanatic. He never actually wrestled, but you ran the very real risk of bodily harm simply by sitting next to him during a televised match. And this took place many moons ago, so although wrestling was still relatively rehearsed, then at least it didn't contain the shock content so common in today's wrestling shows. I'd have quite likely been maimed for life back then. This fellow would leap up off the sofa and mimic FatHead's astounding moves all the while shouting words of encouragement to his hero. And yes, this was in a living room, not the stadium.

And speaking of living rooms, how about the noisy music coming from your next-door neighbour's house? That can be a massive irritant. How can they stand it in the same room? You could complain to the city or town authorities, but you still have to reside next to each other. Ditto with the big arguments. And there's plenty of that takes place. If it's not the kids screaming at each other, it's possibly the kids and parents screaming at each other or perhaps just the parents themselves in a free for all. Arguing about the kids. Although these examples mostly take place behind closed doors, some people obviously forget that even the best of homes can't shut out certain noise levels.

Apparently statistics would indicate that there are a large number of folks in various age groups that quite enjoy roaming about their dwellings in the buff. A.K.A. their birthday suit or in other words stark naked. Now in all fairness, to each his own. But my goodness, at least make certain the curtains are drawn and please do not ever take out the trash in that state of undress.

There's a civic responsibility here that would dictate no one has the right to severely traumatize a fellow human being, either intentionally or unintentionally. Some buffs simply should not be of the opinion that otherwise innocent, modest people would ever want the opportunity to be offered a free rear-view shot of Mr. RolyPoly's ample non-covered over-the-hill behind on trash day. But hey, so long as the curtains are drawn, noise levels are down and everyone's happy, do what you wish - behind closed doors.

# Never Say Never

The human species possesses a relatively short memory span. We cuss our less popular politicians antics until election time, then immediately re-elect them. Unreal. Almost as bad as willingly deciding to change homes.

When we moved to the Crowsnest Pass from Lethbridge, it was an intensely busy move. One tends to accumulate a lot of stuff over 20 years. We completely renovated our place in the Pass. It was a cozy little nest. But it had limited office space. No matter, we'd make do. Not doing that "move-thing" again for many years. "Most certainly not" said the wrinkled, missing-tooth, slightly bulbous liar. As he and his mate browsed the local real estate scene.

Hey, lets check out this place. Just take a quick look. Nothing serious. Hmmm, maybe we'll touch base with a realtor and see if he thinks our place will even sell in this current market. Two days later, we'd put a down payment on the new place, had an offer on our existing place and needed to be out of our place and into the new place in three weeks.

Major stress immediately set up shop. Complete with night sweats, nightmares and the rarely experienced, but exceedingly effective daymares. Slightly distracted, I once deposited the cheese jar into the sink instead of the fridge and poured coffee cream into one of the juice glasses at breakfast. The worst possible scenarios to completely destroy our docile lifestyle were played out like many broken records in my mind. There were entire flocks of "what-ifs" swooping, diving and otherwise endlessly distressing me.

We needed to build a shed. The timeline would be tight. Our contractor said he could do it. If it didn't rain. It rained. My thumping heart was now trying to bore a hole through my chest in a futile quest to escape from any more adverse "oh-my-gosh-what-next" reactions.

The outfit that owned our new place kindly let us move in some of our house stuff. Little twinges of "hey-didn't-we-just-do-this?" memories were cropping up to further torment my already tortured mind. Great gobs of "stuff" were being drawn out of nooks and corners. It was purely unbelievable. Where had all this stuff come from? We'd gotten rid of mammoth amounts of stuff when we moved here from Lethbridge. I came up with a theory, yet to be tested and proven. "Stuff" reproduces. Put two compatible "stuffs" together and in no time, you'll be the proud owner of an entire herd of "stuffs". These "stuff" blighters will put any self-respecting rabbits to shame. But I digress.

We made many trips over to the new place and both vehicles were loaded to the hilt with boxes of all sizes. The new neighbours were supremely entertained. We promised them the best was yet to come. These umpteen dozen trips were only a teaser.

Our bodies ached. Even my eyebrows were stiff. Friends and family helped us in the big move. We're here --- surrounded by "stuff" and unable to even move about in the gluttonous shed. "Never again" said we to each other.

## My Body Thermostat Is Kaput

It was downright chilly. Not bitterly cold, but nonetheless a tad tough on this body. You'd think I'd still be acclimatized from all those years of experiencing harsh Saskatchewan winters (back when winters were really harsh) to the extent this bit of cold weather would be deemed only a minor inconvenience. Unfortunately my body didn't agree. It chattered in disapproval.

My son had been drawn for a moose tag west of Cochrane, Alberta. I accepted an invitation to join him for a three-day hunt where we'd stay in their little trailer. These outings are always a highlight for me. A combination of walking in the morning and riding on an all terrain vehicle (ATV) on existing cut lines in the afternoon through breathtaking mountain landscapes is good for the constitution. I had a deer tag, but was mostly interested in just getting out for a bit of adventure.

We left Cochrane early Monday morning amid light snowfall and temperatures in the low minus Celsius. Camp was setup and the furnace in the little trailer fired up. I was in my element. A tough, seasoned outdoorsman who thrived on cold weather and hardship. Bundled up and toting my trusty rifle, we struck out on a trek in search of the mighty moose. Stream crossings were a little harrowing, but I was full of energy and breathed deeply of the crisp mountain air. An hour or so later and dang it, this up and down terrain was getting a little tiring. My gun obviously needs to go on a diet. It never used to weigh this much.

Eventually we arrived empty-handed back at camp. A quick lunch and off we go on an ATV. Up and down, side to side, over rocks, skidding down steep trails in search of a mighty moose track. (Tracks in themselves don't make for good eating, but are indicative of potential larger snacks.) There was a slight breeze. It was cool on the face, hands and feet. When we stopped for periodic rests, various parts of my body would seize up or vibrate in protest. My teeth began to chatter. It was deemed wise not to let my upper denture turn loose during this chatter. The campsite looked good, even in the dark.

We fired up a great supper in the little trailer. Perry brewed up a healthy outdoor fire in the hopes we'd sit outside and enjoy the evening. My mind was willing, but my body said it was quite fine just staying in the trailer. Unfortunately bodily demands do dictate that quick outings may be required regardless. Our bathroom facilities in this case were comprised of the entire great outdoors. Six layers of clothing make the word "quick" obsolete.

Heat rises. The upper portion of the trailer was toasty from the heat generated by the propane furnace. The floor area was rather chilly. But hey, we had sleeping gear galore. The first night was fine. The next morning it was still snowing and temperatures were even lower. We decided to look for tracks from the truck. Nothing. Another big lunch and off once more on the ATV. That darned thing was determined to buck me off on steep trails. It was a wrestling match. By days end both Perry and I were chattering. Big fire and a big supper.

My truck thermometer said minus 18 Celsius at bedtime.

I couldn't get warm that night. Sleeping gear was heaped on my body. It kept slipping off. My shoulder ached. Goofy quad. My leg ached. Goofy quad. I fell asleep only to awake with an incredibly sore ear. It had somehow got bent and I'd slept on it in this position for a couple of hours. Massaging my sore ear while putting on additional clothes at 3:00 AM gave cause to contemplation that I hoped it would spring back to its original shape. Images of dogs with one cocked ear and one droopy ear were vivid. My bladder said it could sure use a little relief. Forget it said I and snuggled back for a bit more fitful sleep.

Upon arising at 6:00 AM for the final mornings hunt, my truck thermometer said minus 23 Celsius. Everything in the upper level of the trailer was thankfully toasty and dry, where our clothing and boots had spent a most restful night. We quit hunting at noon that day and never did fill the moose tag. This ex-tough, ex-seasoned outdoorsman is now sitting at home typing on a computer in a warm house wondering exactly when, where and how his body thermostat went kaput.

# Wisdom

My little Webster defines wisdom as sound judgment and sagacity; prudence; learning or erudition. Sagacity is defined as quickness of discernment; shrewdness; high intelligence. Erudition is defined as learning; knowledge gained by study; scholarship. A side note -- - above erudition is the word eructation defined as the act of belching. My wisdom is obviously expanding rapidly even as this article is being written. Heck, I might possibly even be accused of eructating erudition.

So - if you're anything like me, my definition of wisdom was associated with age. In other words older people were always considered much wiser than me. I valued their advice and looked forward to the day when I might have half that wisdom. But there's a glitch. The older I'm getting the quicker the realization that I really don't know much at all. This poses an obvious dilemma. I'll never become a fountain of wisdom.

But there appears to be a threshold that one crosses where others suddenly do consider them wise. For whatever reason, I'm starting to encounter that threshold and it's scaring me. My hair is turning grey and in forty-four years I'll be one hundred years old. That must be the deciding factor. "Look he's got grey hair and getting on in age." Occasionally people now ask me to speak in front of other people.

Many years ago, I remember sitting and listening to people speak in front of others and thinking this person sure must be wise to attain this honour. Now it's "oh boy, is this ever scary - what the heck am I going to say"? Those speakers from not so long ago likely felt the same way. It's a sobering revelation. I'm getting older, but realize there's simply too much to learn about worldly matters in one lifetime.

Simple things elude me. I still don't know how they get that caramel into the caramel bar, but certainly wouldn't admit that to a querying youngster. You're pretty much forced to act wise. Ditto with deeper issues such as "why don't both socks get a hole at the same time"? Or "why do they call a wiener in a bun a hot dog"? (Aha, bet you thought I never knew that one? In 1906 a cartoonist drew a dachshund – aka sausage dog – in a bun. I looked that up. A decidedly wise move.)

The old fallback is relating stories. Like proverbs they can quote an example from which your listeners can draw upon for sage advice. A prime example relates to the small scar on my chin. Years ago, my grandmother had sent me uptown to pick up a turkey she'd ordered. Per usual, I was hurrying and running flat out. The usually sedate top step of the veranda took a mean streak and leaped forth to send me sprawling. Fortunately the turkey intervened and wedged itself between my chin and the veranda floor. After regaining consciousness, my jaw and I staggered into the kitchen and presented grandmother with her turkey. She wondered why I was so wobbly and unusually quiet. I was seeing whirling stars and my entire jaw area was shocked into temporary paralysis. The lesson in this story is abundantly clear. Youngsters, even ones in small towns, should never be allowed to run with turkeys. Especially frozen ones.

The image of me rocking slowly in an old wicker chair on the veranda whilst serenely gazing off into the sky and offering up invaluable tidbits of practical advice to young adults is fading. In its place is a wrinkled up squinty-eyed me sitting in a rocking chair asking a young adult how to look up erudition on my huge-key laptop. This wisdom thing isn't all it's cranked up to be.

# When I Grow Up

Decked out in a cowboy hat, toy gun and holster, complete with ragweed horse, I was a sight to behold. Cut quite a dashing figure even at age ten or so. Roy Rogers had even sent me a signed photo of Roy, Dale and Trigger, so there was no doubt that I was a bona fide cowboy. Heck, Roy even knew that. Mom was a bit more of a doubter. I was reasonably certain cowboys never had all those restrictions, like "time-to-go-bed" or "don't-you-dare-talk-like-that-to-me-young-man". Yep, this cowboy life was going to be a tough road.

In my early teen years I rather fancied some of the rock and rollers like Ricky Nelson and Buddy Holly. So I took up guitar playing. But using a steel slider bar for chording, not fingering the chords. It was somewhat different, but good rockers were radical anyway. Then I found country music. And thought my steel bar wasn't realistically countrified. So now I had to learn the other guitar style. Never really got past chording and wailing though. Yep, this singing career was going to be a tough way to make a living.

In grade eleven I realized that one really should move beyond shooting at gophers and tin cans with a slingshot. There had to be more to life. But what should I do? Maybe attend university and get a degree in engineering? Build huge bridges in Africa or Europe. Have a chauffeur and a villa complete with servants. Or maybe I could become a fish and wildlife officer? Ride through parks on a horse, packing a firearm and grappling with dangerous poachers in life and death situations. Protecting a deer. Yep, just deciding what I'd be in the world was going to be a tough deal.

Immediately after graduation from grade twelve, I applied for a job with the Saskatchewan government and became a surveyor. But this was only a temporary thing. I was reasonably certain a chauffeur was still awaiting my arrival somewhere over in Europe. Ten years later, I departed from that job and headed westward with Dear-at-Heart, our two boys, a dog and among our other belongings, my slingshot. The west was where one could find fame and fortune. I would become a famous builder of great things and rise up to become a highly sought-after CEO. Yep, things were moving along nicely.

Twenty years later we were in Lethbridge, Alberta and I was employed by a great long-established conservation organization. The work was personally gratifying and our boys were nearing the stage where they'd soon be leaving home. Our house would be empty. On a clear day you could see the Rocky Mountains from Lethbridge. The mountains called softly and promised tranquility, small town living and a slower pace. I would become a writer of great repute out there and achieve national and international acclaim. Grow a beard and sport a ponytail. Yep, this could be the big one.

Eventually we sold our home in Lethbridge and moved to the Crowsnest Pass, Alberta. Downsized significantly. Bought a small house on a small lot. Started writing full-time. Tried growing a beard, but found it too itchy and kept cutting it off. My hair was getting far too sparse for sporting any semblance of a respectable ponytail. Many people thought we'd gone overboard. Left a perfectly good job for a writing career? Hey, we'd be fine. Stock markets were booming. Yep, this writing career was tough, but we were doing reasonably well.

The stock markets have plummeted. My ponytail and beard is only wishful thinking. Writing a blockbuster novel is a rather daunting task. But corporate writing and some other work in combination with column writing, book writing, book signing events and so on keeps us quite busy. Dear-at-Heart has taken up pottery and oil painting. She does marvelous work. We have a leased-site on a lake in nearby B.C., where we keep our trailer and small boat year around. The lake is loaded with Kokanee, which is basically a freshwater salmon. We've readjusted our outlook on life. Freedom 75 is the realistic target for full retirement. Life's pretty darned good. My old slingshot hangs on a pegboard in the garage. I'd try and shoot a can, but the ancient tire-rubber might snap. Yep, someday I'm going to have to decide what I want to be when I grow up.

# Sociably Acceptable Teeth

Another craze is upon us. Toothpaste companies are scrambling to ensure the message that their product will offer the ultimate in whiter teeth is loud and clear. And some companies are offering various gizmos that will allow you the erstwhile consumer to supremely whiten your teeth right in the comfort of your home. And these ads would have you believe the gizmos are much more effective then just toothpaste. Oh boy, here we go again. The "socially-acceptable" merry-go-round that never ends and this time it's targeting our teeth.

My "pearly-whites" have suffered many indignities over the years. Too much soda pop and chocolate bars as a youth pretty much trashed the upper row. They were yanked out many moons ago and replaced with what used to be termed "false-teeth". Deemed politically incorrect, this term that basically implied "fraudulent" was eventually replaced with the word "dentures".

There is an astounding array of toothpastes gracing store shelves. This vast selection simply confuses me. Not only do the manufacturers make the boxes and squeeze tubes look incredibly attractive, but also the concoction itself. Multi-coloured pastes of various flavours spew forth from the tubes. Each are said to possess qualities that will not only protect and whiten your teeth, but also attract members of the opposite sex. They'll be smitten by simply one glimpse of your pearly-whites.

To prove that point some ads feature the usual generic stunningly beautiful girl passing nearby a tanned handsome man when alas, a glance at one of their teeth causes immediate rejection. These ads are so effective that after wiping a tear from my eye, I've immediately gone to the garage and buffed my upper denture on the grinding wheel.

Upon my return "Dear-at-Heart" was momentarily blinded by the resultant flash of light from a hearty smile. She also wondered about the unique odour now wafting about my entire body. Admittedly the silicone spray I'd so cunningly added during the buffing process was a tad overwhelming. But man where those teeth smooth and shiny. The only downside came when trying to eat a pistachio. Those slippery teeth sent it rocketing off across the living room like a miniature missile launcher.

Sensitive teeth are also addressed by the use of certain toothpastes. At one time there were very few toothpastes that directly touted their soothing use for those with overly sensitive teeth. This must have been a lucrative business. There's now a whole heap of companies offering toothpastes with these unique qualities. Bad enough that one even needed toothpaste for sensitive teeth, since you were kind of admitting to being a wimp. On the plus side though at least now there's some price competition on these toothpastes for sensitive teeth. It was tough enough on me being dubbed Sir Wimp, let alone broke to boot.

One thing is certain. More toothpaste varieties with unique qualities to attract consumers will always be evolving. That's a given. I'm constantly amazed at the fact how this continues and not only with toothpaste. Maybe it's only a new package or a re-labelling, but somehow and someway we're almost guaranteed that a new version of most consumer items will eventually be offered.

I'd like to see a package containing a variety of toothpastes in small tubes that could address almost every common mental occasion. Similar to those scented oils, they might possess mood-altering characteristics. If you'd had a particularly bad day you could brush with a "happy & so-sleepy" paste before retiring for the night. If you knew a particular day was going to be highly stressful, you could brush with an "oh-I'm-so-very-mellow" paste in the morning. And so on. But regardless it's quite obvious from these ads that your teeth will determine your very future in life. Never mind the cavities. Socially acceptable teeth are a must.

# Those Iffy Veggies

Many polite eaters are also accomplished liars. Foodstuffs that are served when one accepts dinner invitations or orders a restaurant plate may actually be on your "yuk-that's terrible" list. And although you may have some control over this at home, going beyond your own kitchen can leave you vulnerable. In my case many cooks obviously have an obscene sense of humour for an abundance of broccoli often adorns the dinner plate.

Who ever deemed broccoli as edible food anyway? Apparently and like many of our foodstuffs, this too was of European descent. Approximately two hundred years ago, it sneaked its way into many North America households and a wayward batch eventually landed up in mom's kitchen. Mom was adamant that broccoli was good for you and by golly gee whiz, her kids were going to eat it.

I was the eldest kid. Trying to pull rank though was futile. Although it was a well-known fact throughout select areas of a certain house in south-eastern Saskatchewan that oatmeal cookies met and exceeded all of the recommended food group criteria, I still needed to eat my broccoli. Alas, to this very day I cannot look at a wad of broccoli with the remotest sense of fondness.

A few of us recently went out for supper and ordered a variety of dishes. Stir fries, hot pots, noodle combos and so on. It promised to be a feast. When it came, every dish was laden with broccoli. It was ridiculous.

And broccoli takes up a lot of room. Mushrooms took a hit.

Many people will attempt to disguise certain "iffy" foods. Cheese is a popular mask. A combination of that orange colour and the fact most people generally like melted cheese helps to ease some cauliflower diner's discomfort. As humans we're conditioned to being easily tricked from early childhood.

Mushy, green baby food is the height of deviousness. It not only looks horrible, but it smells equally bad. Now granted some of that fruity baby food actually does taste good. But by gosh couldn't the makers of this stuff have a bit more creativity? A swooping spoon of mushy peas going "zoom, zoom" followed by "mm, good" doesn't really cut it as a bundle of truth. You're not being a good role model when you resort to fibbing to your child at that early age. "Mm, good" - yeah right.

It's intriguing to think about who originally determined some of these "iffy" veggies were good for you in the first place. Someone had to start the ball rolling. Us humanoids are notorious followers so all it would take is one shot of erroneous "hand-me-down" veggie advice and two hundred years later, we're still being told the same tale. Possibly even now teaching the same tale in the popular "I-don't-care-just-get-them-to-eat-their-veggies" schools. And all because someone's great-great-great-great-grandma with failing eyesight goofed up and put broccoli in the wrong pot. Pride prevented the family from ever acknowledging they'd just eaten grandpa's poultice and to this very day I'm still paying for that error.

Portion of a Large Puffball Mushroom

# Almost Rich

This had to be the one - we were so close that I could almost smell the money. Dutifully dissecting the package and trying mightily to decipher what sticky seals got placed where, whilst also trying to avoid ordering the book, the package was finally ready to mail back in the "no" envelope. Another stamp and a bit of personal time was the primary investment. The possibilities were huge. Another effort completed toward the endless pursuit of trying to win some money.

Fortunately we've never kept track of all the postage stamp money invested in these sweepstake and other contest entries. That amount would likely be surprising. But your odds of winning increase dramatically if you actually enter the contest. At least that should be the rationale. However to date, we haven't won anything monetarily wise. A wristwatch that was deemed of high quality was once won, but upon close inspection the "high quality" thing is much like the saying "beauty is in the eyes of the beholder". In other words, it didn't really look all that great in my eyes.

Lottery tickets are a biggie these days. We've known some folks that have won a large amount of money and of course I'm somewhat envious of their having attained this "new-money". What never ceases to amaze me is that for every winner who honestly is in need of this money, there appears to be many more who are quite affluent to begin with and are now stuck with this dastardly extra money. This would be a nice dilemma.

Unfortunately or perhaps fortunately we never buy lottery tickets on a regular basis. Every once in awhile, I'll buy one or two, faithfully check if we're a winner, note that of course not and then not buy any again for another year. That strategy significantly reduces our chances of ever winning. But my theory is that some people are never meant to ever win anything. Their main role is to contribute to these lotteries and just be content with that. Now in all fairness some of these sweepstakes lotteries do support good causes, so in that sense a contribution can be viewed simply as a contribution. If one wins, that's a bonus.

Those promotional sweepstakes are the ones that get me. It doesn't cost you anything up front, unless you order the product being promoted. Which of course is the real intent of the sweepstakes offer in the first place. In fact the accompanying letter and even the return "no" envelope is carefully designed to make you feel like a real deadbeat if you don't order the product. The bonus offers alone attached to a "yes" reply are so numerous that you're left reeling in breathless anticipation of not only having all that money, but a new car to boot. Wow, one needs to take a walk around the block just to bolster up the old nerves and stick with the "no" envelope.

Occasionally though we have ordered a product if it was of interest. That simple act appears to unleash a torrent of sweepstakes offers that makes you certain beyond all doubt that millionaire status is inevitable. I've contemplated using one or two of these "almost-there" letters as collateral for a hefty bank loan, but wasn't entirely certain if the bank shared my optimism. The letters that come ahead of time forewarning you that a package of significant importance is forthcoming are almost scary. Then the package arrives. It's plum full of sticky seals, certificates and sample cheques bearing your name.

The first time this happened, I darn near quit work. The second time this happened, I put off buying another vehicle for a few months. The third time this happened, I thought the watch looked a little cheaper than the promotion hype. The forth time this happened; I left the package sitting for a week before opening. Now as I'm getting older and looking ahead at retirement years, these sweepstakes are once again of interest. They may play a significant role in our retirement portfolio. In fact, I'm reasonably certain this last entry will propel us into monetary bliss. Contemplating what to wear for the cheque presentation ceremony must certainly mean I'm almost rich.

# Low Morels & Loose Clothing

In the mountainous terrain around our home, there's a multitude of wildlife to be found, plus great stream and lake fishing. The massive fires of last year were devastating and several of our normally green mountainsides look quite barren. But a certain breed of mushroom apparently thrives in select areas of these burns.

Dear-at-Heart announced that she was going shroom picking with a friend of hers. Approximately three hours later she arrived back home with a pail of what can be best described as a herd of downright ugly looking little fat dome-shaped thingamajigs. They were deeply wrinkled and of varying sizes with dark colouration. I was rather intimidated by their disgusting appearance.

But Dear-at-Heart was obviously enthused over this bountiful harvest. She was now also a wealth of information on these ugly wrinklies. Morel mushrooms said she --- supposedly unbelievably tasty and in high demand. There were even professional pickers and buyers currently out in woods. We were going picking said she. I was still in awe over the fact someone, somewhere, had actually eaten one of these ugly things to even know if they were edible. Probably had one with their lobster, which made it a double ugly whammy.

Now one cannot feasibly eat a whole bucket of these at a sitting. So they'd need to be preserved. I swung into action. Well actually my one finger swung into action.

The ever-dependable Internet provided the always-predictable information-overload on morel mushrooms. There were pages upon pages of recipes, picking tips and so on. Over five hundred easy ways to cook and preserve morel mushrooms. We only needed one good recipe. It was overwhelming.

One suggestion said to use only butter for sautéing. Any other option such as margarine would be akin to a direct insult to this outstanding morsel. Now that was intriguing. And by gosh they did taste good. A mushroom picking date was set with another couple. It was hidey-ho and off we go to a burn site.

Dear-at-Heart glommed on to a morel right off the bat and did the standard show'n tell for us ignoramus. I made a mental note that these things looked even worse in their natural setting then they did in the pail. To begin with we were in an area that had recently suffered the adverse effects of a severe forest fire. It was a tad sooty.

Unless you hit the mother lode, it was mighty slim pickings. You'd meander along looking for little wrinkled thingamajigs poking up out of the soot. Once found, you'd lean down and cut off the upper part complete with some stem but leaving the root intact. Up and down the rolling terrain and over and through sooty deadfalls was tiring. Leaning against a tree left you tarnished with a distinct black hue. The presence of bear droppings gave rise to troubling thoughts. Peering upward was detrimental to the search. My joints were audibly creaking. But we persevered. And gave thanks for low morels and loose clothing.

A Batch of Morel Mushrooms

# Dessert Anyone?

Mom generally always made a dessert to serve with our meals on the farm. I was henceforth spoiled for life. But back then we actually did some physical labour. And I was a skinny kid right up until departing the farm at the ripe old age of 18. For several years thereafter desserts were still required to properly round out a meal.

Then a peculiar thing started to happen. Those desserts must not have been digesting properly. They were heaping up in my stomach and creating an obvious bulge. The doctor said he'd seen similar problems, but never fully understood the reason, until hearing my explanation. He kindly acknowledged my self-diagnosis, but basically left the solution in my hands saying there were no pills available to combat that problem. He did try to make a joke out of my dilemma by suggesting I cut down on my desserts. We both shared a hearty laugh at that one. Yep, that was one funny doctor.

Homemade pies are probably one of my favourite desserts. They come in such a variety of fillings and toppings. Rhubarb pie either alone or mixed with fruit was just way too good. Especially with that nice brown piecrust lovingly created by mom using the old wood stove. Apple pie is super, but then so is a mincemeat, raisin or cherry pie. Even lemon or coconut pie topped off with a fluffy meringue top is hard to beat. Heck, come to think of it, they're all great.

But apple crisp ranks right up there too. Or even blueberry crisp. It's hard to eat only one helping of any breed of crisp, especially when topped off by a hearty scoop of real ice cream. (My definition of real ice cream means the creamy tasting stuff that doesn't turn into flaky ice-chips immediately upon exposure to fresh air.)

Now cakes are another biggie for desserts. But it's funny how most regular cake is generally only eaten with a lunch or with a cup of coffee. Unless of course it's a birthday cake or some other special occasion cake. Then it becomes a full-fledged dessert and usually topped off with ice cream. I used to like birthday cake when the kids were still living at home. The odds of snagging a coin were reasonably good. Now it's just a cake with a zillion candles.

But there sure are a variety of cakes. The possibilities are endless. Matrimony (where the heck did that term come from?) cake is very good, but it's a humbling cake. Try as you might, you do make a mess when eating a matrimony cake. Unless it's a gooey matrimony cake, which generally means the cook made a mistake in the making of it.

Cookies are another favourite. And again the limits are boundless. Its fun to note how some of the commercially made cookies are now touting the fact their particular cookie is over loaded with chocolate chips or nuts, whatever. Some of those triple-dosed models look like they're simply a cluster of chocolate chips being held together by a minimal amount of sticky coloured flour paste. Oatmeal or peanut butter cookies are just great.

Dainty desserts are fine, but some of these are so sweet my teeth hurt just by looking at them. You pretty much have to mix and match, in order to retain some semblance of sugar-control. A mince tart and one of those ultra-sweet mint-chocolate squares need to be combined with a slice of rather tame looking white-cake. It's ironic that they'll offer these mega-selections of sweet desserts in a setting that generally dictates you need to sit still for the remainder of the evening. You've just completely overdosed on fidget-fuel and now need to be quiet. The organizers need to allow a half-hour of potent polka time right after dessert.

Unfortunately I have had to cut back on my dessert intake. Dear-at-Heart does periodically make all of the above-mentioned goodies, so I'm not totally deprived. The desserts still heap up and create a bulge. So even though that doctor was only joking around, I have had to cut back. Slightly. Dear-at-Heart made some scones yesterday. They're very good. Also.

# Let There Be Light

The coal-oil lamp that was left burning overnight at the head of the stairs was a welcome comfort through my years as a farm youngster. If you happened to awake suddenly due to some disturbance such as Spot, your trusty dog and bedfellow, yipping at a rabbit in his sleep the soft light would quickly soothe you back into blissful slumber. I really never noticed that distinctive coal-oil fuel smell until after leaving the farm following high school and then periodically returning.

The coal-oil lantern was also a tremendous asset for night time excursions. Whether putting up the horses after arriving home near nightfall, milking the cows, heading down to the biffy or slipping out to the granary on a cold winters night to hack off a piece of venison for toasting over the fire, those lanterns were and still are pretty darn practical. Not much can go wrong with them. No flimsy mantles to break. Trim the wick periodically and that's about it.

It's quite amazing how we're now so accustomed to light. Living in the city or even in towns with ever-active streetlights, one seldom gets to experience real darkness any more. In fact it gets to the point where darkness can be a tad spooky. But there's nothing quite so spectacular as seeing the sky come alive on a clear night when you're surrounded by absolute darkness. It's breathtaking. Generally though, unless you're well away from civilization, there's a light coming from somewhere nearby.

Even modern day camping offers all-night lighting. Those little solar-powered lights are the big rage now. You see them perched on posts in both campsites and residential yards. They're pretty practical. Once you've paid for the purchase our sun does the rest.

In the course of my multi-faceted career, I've encountered a few fairly affluent individuals who were quite willing to pay excessive amounts of money simply to have a place where no nearby yard lights were visible. No kidding. And one person was even suggesting he could possibly buy out a neighbour, thus eliminating his light. That's a tad extreme.

So in the absence of trusty old lanterns, we now have modern-day flashlights. In my day, we also had flashlights, but batteries were not quite as affordable as coal oil. Now we've got an absolute glut of flashlights and other outdoor-type portable lighting. Too many. By the time I get around to using one of the less popular models in our stock there's a reasonably good chance the battery may be dead. And there's also a good chance those batteries won't be on hand. Cause there's now a gazillion battery-types on the market. All shapes, sizes and uses.

A quick rundown of our portable lights offered the following. The big square flashlight takes a big square heavy battery. Good reliable outdoor light for biffy treks on campouts. Relatively easy to spot unfriendly eyes in the dark. Then we have four or five regular type flashlights that take two regular type batteries each. These don't get used that often, so the batteries are generally corroded lumps when needed.

There's one long, sleek, black flashlight that takes four regular type batteries. Solid, heavy and far-reaching. If the unfriendly eyes in the dark ever materialized into an all out attack, this flashlight could serve as a club-like weapon. I also have a cloned miniature of this big light. It's a handy little fellow and throws a remarkably bright light. But of course does take different size batteries. This little light has a case that can be strapped to your belt.

There's a headlamp that takes a really weird battery but is a surprisingly useful unit. Both your hands are left free to do whatever task is at hand. The headlamp swivels up and down and is adjustable for brightness. The head straps are comfortable and of high quality. This little unit would have been great for night time cow milking way back in my younger years.

We received a Christmas gift of a portable lantern that is truly a marvel of modern-day technology. It has two short fluorescent tubes and runs off an internal rechargeable battery. You can turn on one tube or both. There's the option of a reflective mirror. This unit can be charged off your regular house current or through a lighter connection off your car battery.

We also have a coal-oil lamp, an old style coal-oil lantern and a small jug of coal oil on hand. Just in case.

# Turkey Kinfolk

I've always suspected but have never been able to prove that most of us possess recognizable turkey genes in our physical make-up. And I don't mean when we directly call someone a "turkey" or refer to them as in "what-a-turkey". No, I mean some of us actually bear certain physical resemblances and mannerisms common to old "gobble-gobble".

Apparently wild turkeys were first discovered in America and about 500 years ago domesticated versions came into being. Now supposedly a case of mistaken identity resulted in the bird even being called a turkey. This American bird was introduced to Europe about 400 years ago. The English thought it was the same bird they called a turkey that was shipped from Africa to England via the country of Turkey. Although the mistake was realized apparently the name has remained.

Turkey mortality rates increase dramatically during Thanksgiving, Christmas and New Years. We then eat vast quantities of the birds in a variety of ways. Culinary creativity abounds and we become virtual turkey-laden blimps. Is it so unusual to suspect that over the span of 500 years in practicing this excessive turkey consumption within the bounds of such few special occasions there could result an accidental infusion of turkey genes? Aha - got you thinking. And therein lies the basis of my theory.

That flap of skin under a turkey's chin is called a wattle. I've always had a small wattle. Over the years my wattle has developed significantly to the point that it's now quite prominent. My concern is that if it continues to develop and I'm blessed with living to a ripe old age, it could feasibly cover the upper one-third of a necktie. Since I'm not really a necktie person, my wattle could perhaps be stuffed inside my shirt collar. In fact this may be the very reason that some older people wear shirts buttoned right to the top.

Male turkeys are likely to have additional wattles on their neck. My neck must have given birth to an entire colony of wattles during one particular night. And they're gaining prominence. Thankfully though it doesn't appear that everyone develops these wattles. And I'm not really into the world of cosmetics. Perhaps an anti-wattle cream is already being marketed.

Wild turkeys can fly. Domesticated turkeys can't fly primarily due to the fact they weigh about twice the weight of a wild turkey. As a youngster, I was relatively wild and could run like the wind. Then I became more mature, married and in a sense domesticated. My weight has increased significantly to the extent I can no longer run as before. See that? The resemblance is uncanny.

Male turkeys strut about trying to attract females. They'll fight among themselves over access to females. Ditto with young men. The flap of skin hanging over a turkey's beak is called a caruncle or snood. It turns bright red during courtship or when the turkey is upset. A slang term sometimes refers to your nose as a snout or snoot. Change the "t" to "d" and we have snood. Some people's noses (snoods) do turn quite red when they're upset. Unfortunately I can't accurately

comment on the courtship bit.  Never really took notice.
But hey, aren't all these similarities neat?

Turkey's are also omnivores.  My little Webster defines
"omnivorous" as all devouring; eating food of every
kind.  In other words turkeys will eat virtually anything.
And that's definitely me.  Which raises one question.  If
my theory that turkeys are indeed some remote
semblance of kinfolk, but I'm eating them - hmmm -
time for some contemplation.  And a turkey sandwich.

## Eeek Mail

The chain letter was addressed to my e-mail but it also included a huge number of other e-addresses. The sender said this chain letter possessed unbelievable powers. But you need to immediately forward it on to ten other people in your e-mail circuit. If you don't do this, your dear sender will be emotionally and financially crushed. I never liked those envelope sent chain letters. I absolutely detest these e-mail versions.

Then there are those who are bound and determined to disrupt the use of legitimate e-mail. They're obviously bored and clearly mentally impotent on the social contribution front. Viruses are an unwanted plague that prey on both the suspecting and unsuspecting. Even the most cautious users are vulnerable. If only these virus creators would put what must be some talent, to good use.

Then there are the spammers. My goodness, what is that all about? If you never had low self-esteem beforehand, just try taking to heart a few of these messages. Your inadequacies will range from the most intimate physical details all the way to needing a cable television filter. Those that adhere to the conspiracy theory will be looking for hidden cameras in their bathroom.

We have a spam blocker on our e-mail. A few spam messages still manage to get through. If you want to report these as spam to your network, each one has to be forwarded. I don't profess to even having a clue how these spam blockers work. You can't block everyone, so on our system we just put in options to block any obvious spammers.

Our cellular phone can also read e-mail messages. When spam messages appear on that little gizmo, it's a real pain. Deleting each of them takes a while and that little cellular screen is a definite squint-challenge for my aging, inadequate eyes.

Expectations have also hit a new high with business e-mail. When someone sends you a request, you'd best get on that right now. With competitors lurking in the background, it becomes all the more urgent. If you can't fulfill your client's needs in a timely manner someone else sure as heck will do it. The definition of "timely" is a grey area.

Digital e-images are neat. They can also be a pain. You'll receive a message from a close friend that you can hardly wait to open. You wait for it to download. Twenty minutes later it's on 1 %. A quick estimate says you'll get to view that thing in about a week. Then your computer mercifully says that file is just way too big. It may contain only one humungous image.

You don't have what they call high speed internet service. You're on what they call a dial-up network. In today's fast-paced e-world, that means you're a turtle. On the plus side, turtles have protective shells. You'll need one when your next message that did download tells you what this tiny little pill can accomplish. And why you desperately need it. That's why I now call this "eeek-mail".

# Slivers & Stuff

The ultra-sharp drafting pencil tip entered my lower lip rather sneakily, but immediately gained hurt status. Blood spurted out and the pensive mood that had caused the pencil to even be near my lip in the first place was quickly replaced with a rather surprised "ouch". Dashing off to the bathroom for a quick boo in the mirror confirmed that my lip had indeed been attacked. What I didn't immediately notice was the pencil tip had stayed put in my lip. To this day, I bear the proud scar of a draftsman wounded in the line of duty. A little black lump of pencil lead rests peacefully in my lower lip.

A number of years ago a friend and I were deer hunting in a coulee area landscape south of Lethbridge, Alberta. It was a dry, arid, almost desert-like setting. Cactus plants lay flat against the ground in some spots. At the edge of a rather steep brushy coulee, my friend decided to lob a rock into the brush in the hopes that a deer may have bedded there for the day. "Lob" went the rock; "screech" went Steve. The effort of throwing the rock combined with a steep slope had resulted in his feet shooting out from under him. With unerring accuracy he'd landed smack dap on top of a cactus family. He was in agony and refused all efforts of help on my part in extracting the many embedded spines. Modesty overrode practicality. The ride home was rather prickly.

Bee stings, thistles, thorns, tiny fragments of steel, fishhooks and so on have invaded my body over the years. Plus of course varying sized pieces of wood. I called most all of these slivers and the first line of defence was generally to try and extract the sliver with tweezers. Failing that one would then try and expose the tip of the sliver by use of a needle. Relief was pretty much immediate.

We're putting in a new fence on our little property. The old fence is being removed, new fence-boards cut and shaped, 2 x 4's cut and so on. Gloves are cumbersome during much of this work. My hands are natural attractants for slivers of wood. Normally the slivers simply get absorbed and I quite honestly don't know what happens to them. But occasionally, I get a whopper and do require the traditional treatment of tweezers and possibly needle.

One whopper entered my thumb just above the crease line. Dash off to the house and root out the tweezers. The tip of the sliver comes off but the main chunk of log remains firmly embedded. Oh well, I'll get that later. Time to get that fence built. A small piece of log enters the crease area of a finger on my right hand. Those creases are sensitive little areas. Half-cut already, so the nerves must be sitting right there. Anyhow, most of that sliver comes out. But the big blighter is a problem. I'll get that one out tonight.

My hands aren't as steady as they used to be. Although Dear-at-Heart possesses the hand steadiness of a brain surgeon, I'm rather timid when other people are poking about in an already tender area. The sliver is nowhere to be seen, but is definitely still in there. My waving needle efforts produce a wide range of tiny skin pricks that now looks like some multi-toothed small animal has bit me. No sliver to be found. The next morning my thumb is infected. Time to put on a poultice and see if it will draw the sliver out. Bread, oatmeal, potato; they're all supposedly pretty good. Out with the needle once more and open up the area for the poultice to work on.

The poultice doesn't seem to be working. We're now out at the lake. I'm looking for tweezers in our amply supplied first-aid kit. Scanning the list of items, I spot "splinter forceps". Sure enough, there's something that looks remarkably like tweezers. Out with another needle and those "splinter forceps". By now the original tiny wound looks as if a hefty portion of my thumb had got caught in a meat grinder. Sliver-stress has created excessive hand tremors. It's become a case of practicing needlepoint on my thumb. I give up and put on a dose of antibiotic paste and a band-aid. And go fishing.

The next day my thumb is starting to feel better. There's a lump of scar tissue forming from my probing attempts. Now I'm in a quandary. Was it the "splinter forceps" or the handling of freshly caught fish? Does a Kokanee poultice sound reasonable?

# Putting On the Falsies

It's a social misdemeanour of massive proportions. And those few folks that pride themselves on marching to a different beat are more unusual then usual. Yep, our private worlds and the ones we oft times present socially can certainly be different.

Scenario one. You get a phone call that company's on the way. Well break out the dust cloth and call in the sweepers. Depending on the time of arrival, this can be a most trying experience. The male residents are completely bewildered. The house has always looked great. Heck you could eat off the floor.

But now your better half is dashing about at warp speed, dusting, sweeping. You're strongly advised to bail out of that old sweatshirt into something more "presentable". Goodies magically appear. Now where the blazes did those come from? This is a definite highlight for the males.

Scenario two. You're off to the big reunion. Flat broke, overweight and stressed to the noggins. But by gosh the last thing you want to do is look unsuccessful. So you and 90 % of the other attendees suck in your bellies, put on your finest duds and buy drinks all round.

If you're really desperate, you'll have pre-purchased a big costume jewellery ring and a few cigars. In between coughing fits you can pass around the postcards you got at the second-hand store. And tell them those trips were okay, but there's nothing like home and old friends. With any luck, they'll buy you a drink.

Scenario three. You're going on a date. At age fifty-five. You've been a bachelor all your life. But your well-meaning buddies feel you need a lady friend in your life. It's pretty spooky. Especially for your date.

By the time you leave the house you're having a full identity crisis attack. Gone is the flannel shirt and jeans. Gone are the comfortable shoes. You're dressed up in a fancy silk shirt that's way too chilly. Pants have a crease that you could cut bread with. Your hair is all ruffled up and hard as a rock from the gel your buddies insisted upon. And you smell like a lilac bush. You're terrified and totally uncomfortable. And so is your date. She has buddies too.

Scenario four. You're at an ultra-fancy outing attended by some exceedingly well-off corporate people that fairly ooze success and confidence. The ladies must have cleaned out most of the city's jewellery store stock and are wearing it all. They hold their wine glasses high using two fingers. The men are loud and smell like a barbershop. They're drinking expensive straight liquor with ice. You take some just to also appear sophisticated, but like always it makes you gag.

Waiters bring around trays with tiny mysterious looking little tidbits on them. The impaled goodies aren't much larger then the toothpicks. You eat a couple, but have absolutely no idea what they are. It's hot. You're sweating for many reasons. Putting on the falsies is one of the biggest reasons.

# Compliments

The other day while paying for a fill-up of what is now nearly economically on par with liquid gold (gas), the lady cashier commented on my sweater. She said it looked nice and I thanked her then said my wife had bought it for me. That was an automatic reaction since I wasn't entirely certain how else to respond. After all this was a bar. Oh sure it was a gas bar and it was 11:00 AM and I'm chubby, gray-haired, wrinkled and missing a tooth, but I'm quite in tune to this sort of stuff. In the past 35 years, I've watched a lot of television. Just kidding. Actually it was a nice compliment from a nice lady, but it did get me thinking about "compliments" or the lack thereof.

Ladies will compliment other ladies on their attire or other features without hesitation. Assuming the ladies are on speaking terms to begin with. Otherwise the compliments are likely to be barbed. And the arrows might have possibly been dipped in a large vat of poison. Or so it may sound to the casual ear.

Ladies will also compliment men without hesitation. And it doesn't have to be with overtones of excessive personal interest. Just offering a nice compliment. Like the one I experienced at the bar. (At my age one may tend to exaggerate, simply by leaving out certain aspects of a story - "gas" bar would significantly reduce the mystique.)

But guys complimenting guys on their choice of clothing attire is extremely rare. In fact it can be downright risky. There's a heap of behind-the-scenes perception going on at the best of times in a male's shaky existence.

The last thing you need is Buster telling you your new shirt looks "absolutely-dashing". It's pretty much guaranteed that you'll be looking askance at Buster for the rest of your life. And probably shy away from any situation where the two of you might possibly be alone. Even if you used to be die-hard fishing buddies. And the ice shack is definitely off-limits.

One exception where guys might compliment other guys is on their hunting attire. But that's not really meant as a compliment. More like "hey, where'd you get that camo-shirt? Lots of pockets and the blighter looks like it might be a warm one". The comment really means "lucky dog, sure wish I had a shirt like that one".

Same thing applies to boots. Hunting boots are now a measure of class distinction. Especially if they're a pair of name - brand camouflage, waterproof, lightweight boots specifically designed for hunting and costing what I once paid for a well-used 1962 Chevrolet. These boots automatically propel you into an envious position of high esteem by the hunting fraternity. Not for your excellent choice in footwear, but for your obvious prowess in convincing your better half these boots were going to enhance your success toward securing wild game. Wow, you've got it made.

Hairstyles are also apt to receive ready compliments between lady acquaintances. Some ladies have been known to come right out and say, "I like your hair. That style looks good on you". Men do notice other men's hairstyles, but great gobs of hairy horrors; you would never in your wildest moment come out and say Bubba's hairstyle looked good on him.

The primary reason for checking in the first place was simply to see if your male counterparts were balder or greyer then you. And if not, you would then inwardly contemplate on whether they were using hair growth enhancer or colour assistance. That's it. That's all. If Buster says your cowlick looks cute, he'll be one lonely fisherman.

## Aesthetically Acceptable Thingees

Buying or receiving a gift of new clothing items is exciting. But depending on quality and more often the physical attributes, most of these items are prone to ejecting loose little remnants of their material. Especially until washed several times. Some of my socks must be constructed entirely of tiny lumps of yarn lightly linked together. The inside surfaces of these socks are continually spewing out tiny lumps of yarn right up to the time Dear-at-Heart decrees said sock has lived out its life and is now officially kaput.

Removing a sock at the end of the day can be both a relief and a tad distressing. Your tootsies love the fresh air, but are also apt to be the recipient of some of the little lumpy yarn remnants. These wayward thingees love to nestle in between and under ones toes. And if they're not studiously removed, you can be sure they'll transfer themselves onto the carpet. I used to buy black socks. But we now have a light coloured bedroom carpet. At bedtime and after sock removal, it looked like a zebra was napping on the floor.

Solutions to this problem vary. Removing the carpet in favour of putting in linoleum so as to minimize thingee transfer might be called drastic. A far more reasonable approach is to only buy socks in a colouration that matches the carpet. Removing a small sample of carpet from an inconspicuous corner of the room and taking it with you while sock shopping will ensure a perfect colour match. Just ignore the stares from your fellow shoppers or curious salespeople. This is an exercise in cutting edge practicality, which they may not fully appreciate.

Pet-hairs can also be a nuisance. If one is a die-hard pet owner, it seems that you're blissfully unaware of all these hairs floating about and attaching to everything. But to others it can be a source of irritation. Especially if they unknowingly plunk down on Rover's favourite chesterfield and are wearing some fleecy type of clothing. Copious amounts of black dog hairs on a white sweater or vice versa are rather conspicuous. Some non-pet people are quite sensitive about the issue and can suffer hairy thingee attacks of momentous proportions. Especially if someone inadvertently compliments them on their fashionable bear rug backed sweater. Right after they'd just left Rover's place to attend the social event of the year.

Food thingee attachments like crunchy potato chips are also quite noticeable. Unfortunately many eaters never notice these thingees. Fortunately their spouses usually do.

We recently put a set of new seat covers in our car. They looked quite neat. Kind of shaggy and nicely matched the interior colours. Unfortunately the shag portion was really comprised of several thousand little thingees. Anywhere we'd go, we had to inspect each other's backside to ensure little bright blue thingees hadn't hitched themselves to our clothing. But being exceedingly practical, I've now re-adjusted my entire Honda wardrobe. It's resulted in relatively stress free car riding. Denims and blue thingees are aesthetically acceptable.

# Geezer Angst

The tension is building. As one gets older, one is expected to be a bottomless well of wise advice gleaned from years of real life experience. The questions already thrown your way are ridiculously tough and there are hordes more to come. But you'll persevere. After all, old geezers have been around for centuries.

My little Webster doesn't list "geezer" let alone "old geezer". But other sites refer to "old geezers" as old-timers with salt-of-the-earth qualities. That salt-of-the-earth thing is an appealing definition. Age- wise it seems that anyone over 55 is a probable candidate. That's a sobering thought for an aged youngster like me. I'm right up there in geezerville. Need proof? The candles on my last birthday cake partially scorched our ceiling fan and then set off the smoke alarm - at the house next door.

In the past decade or so, I've come to the realization that for some oddball reason the older I get, there's more things on this great and wonderful earth that absolutely confound me. That doesn't bode well for maintaining old-geezer diamond status. It's causing me angst.

Born and raised in a small farming community, there were always a few old geezers gracing the verandas of houses in our nearby town. In a small community like that, you knew most all of these geezers by name. Heck, you were related to quite a batch of them. And they were indeed wise. I was impressed.

The geezers I knew back then would peer out at the world from beneath bushy white eyebrows and dole out opinions on pretty much anything or anybody. Through astute observation I noted that their knowledge and opinions increased substantially if they'd just returned from the local watering hole. And they were funny. But their humorous opinions weren't always looked upon with favour by their respective spouses. That was a poser for a young impressionable lad like me.

As life marched onward and my wrinkles became more prominent, I came to the realization that from our time of birth we're essentially geezers-in-training. We're continually collecting and storing vast amounts of information from experiences both good and bad. If you're really lucky, you might even learn when it's best to just not say anything. But my brain's connector wires must have already sustained severe corrosion in the memory storage area. Perhaps that's part of the big plan for geezers. Cranky old geezers are generally widely accepted as part of our social hierarchy. That gives me some consolation.

I've also noticed that there are several variations of geezers out there. Some geezers prefer to be loners. Others possess pack instincts. You're most likely to see these pack-friendly geezers congregate at coffee shops. They tend to solve problems of most any magnitude, but really shine when it comes to addressing worldly affairs. The downside is that all these brilliant solutions generally remain within the confines of the pack.

So look out world. Here comes another geezer packed plumb full of knowledge and wanting to share some of it. My eyebrows are getting quite bushy.

A Mighty Hunter at Rest

# Yeahbut

We're all plagued on a daily basis by the mysterious group that prompts those influential "they-say" phrases. Opinionated to the umpteenth degree "they-say" permeates every aspect of our life. Coffee anyone? "They-say" its not good for you. Well, there are other not so mysterious influences out there as well. We've all been subjected to the "yeahbut". And there are a lot of them.

You'll come up with what seems like a great idea. Unfortunately you'll likely communicate this idea elsewhere before initiating it. A "yeahbut" will materialize seemingly out of nowhere to effectively extinguish this burst of enthusiasm. "What? Are you crazy? That'll never work. Give up that idea right now." And 9 times out of 10 you do.

But perhaps the "yeahbut" shouldn't always be taken so seriously. Now granted some ideas are truly hair-brained (now where the heck did that saying ever come from?) and deserve to be promptly extinguished. Other ideas though need to be acted upon. Gosh, we'd still be back in the dark ages if every "yeahbut" had his or her way.

Can you imagine the massive influx of "yeahbut" that surfaced when man first tried to build and operate a flying machine? What if the "yeahbut" had won over? We'd still be trying to hitch up a team of 8 eagles to pull us about on a sun-stiffened buffalo hide. "Yeahbut" how would you ever land that thing? And don't eagles relieve themselves while in flight? Like seagulls do?  See what I mean?  Another great idea shot down.

I've often wondered how many people come up with the same ideas.  Because inevitably someone will say they should do such and such.  But that's as far as it goes.  Then their very idea shows up in a store or catalogue.  They probably got severely yelled at by a "yeahbut" for even thinking their idea was possible.  It's likely the ones that are hard of hearing that eventually get their idea into the working stage.  Hmm - a government-funded study might be in order here.  "Yeahbut" hasn't one already been done?  Oh probably.  Drat, there goes another idea.

This "yeahbut" stuff affects people throughout their employment careers as well.  Many supervisory personnel tend to discourage rather then encourage employees to offer suggestions and ideas.  It may not be intentional, however after hearing "yeahbut" immediately after the past five suggestions, one is likely to just clam up and do their basic job.  And one more truly great idea gets kyboshed.  Fortunately there are many companies today that thrive on their employee's suggestions.

Humans need to be dreamers or visionaries.  If you don't dream of doing certain things, life would be pretty darned boring.  And you'd accomplish zip.  These don't have to be grandiose dreams or visions.  And you don't have to be monetarily rich.  If the accomplishment gives you personal satisfaction, then does anything else truly matter?  Let the "yeahbut" stew and fume all he or she wants.  After all was life really intended to be this serious?  Cause it can be pretty darned short.  And one

thing we all seem to share is that life here on earth does
eventually end. "Yeahbut".

A Nice Day for Fishing

# Diagnosing the Remedies

Apparently if I'm to remain living for any further duration of time, I must immediately cease and desist from any eating, drinking or breathing. That unto itself has caused me a tad of stress, which will apparently also contribute greatly to my demise. Then I'm led to believe that some of the very medicines intended to heal any of my blights might also possibly do me in by their side effects. Well great gobs of goopy grapes, what the heck is a fellow supposed to do? I'm obviously doomed no matter what.

Any way you cut it there must be a conspiracy afloat to get rid of a substantial portion of the human population through an overdose of symptomatic confusion. If you were to move to a remote area without any outside contact, you'd quite possibly live to a ripe old age.

But I unfortunately am attuned to every tidbit of news. And thus am quite aware that the dilemma of chicken egg consumption is still an ongoing battle. My dear departed mother, my grandmother, her mother and her grandmother, plus several generations of chickens were quite fine with this issue. Eggs were served in a number of ways, whenever desired.

I got a wood tick bite the other day. Big deal said I. Probably had over 500 ticks latched on to various parts of my anatomy over the years. This bite festered. My mind cells in charge of medical things did a quick scan of stuff to be worried about and sent a "tick" alert out to the rest of my already overly taxed worry cells. Off to the doctor went I with my little tick bite. Hmmm, said the doc. Maybe we'll prescribe these "just-in-case" pills.

At the pharmacy I received the pill info material. It became apparent that my tick bite was the least of my worries. Perhaps it's a diversionary tactic designed to take your mind off the immediate problem. Because those little pills could feasibly create more potential side effect chaos then if I'd purposely tried to scratch a healthy rattlesnake's nose with my bare big toe. Now I was really worried.

The Internet provides sites where one can get information on nearly any drug or disease. Before you even go near a doctor's office, you can pretty much play "spin-the-bottle" to determine your latest malady. Self-diagnosing a sore leg might put you into a state of extreme distress. On the plus side you'll now finally be able to play doctor, if perchance one of your acquaintances suffers from an ache similar to yours.
It's no small wonder that the bona fide doctors are generally expected to issue a prescription following any visit. Dear Aunt Websavvy knows with absolute certainty she's suffering from a severe lack of up-poof ever since she quit eating her two daily eggs. The harried doctor wearily prescribes a pill. Aunt Websavvy checks the side effects. Now she notices her left elbow is also sore. And it's clearly the doctor's fault.

A Campfire Steak – Hunger Medicine!

# Tire Trauma

Way back when I acquired my first car, a vehicle that had tires possessing any semblance of tread was looked at suspiciously. They were obviously wealthy, but possibly bootleggers by trade. Or else they were simply misguided folks who had inadvertently placed a priority on purchasing good tires versus buying a fine firearm or two or maybe three. Strange people, but wc tolerated them nonetheless.

The word hydroplaning was thought to be directly associated with a flying machine. I now know that it means to lose control of your vehicle on moisture-heavy road surfaces. Back then we called it "wow, that was close" generally followed by "got to get some better tires on the old heap - someday". "Someday" was used quite loosely as it seemed there was always too much month at the end of the money. Tires could wait.

Buying used tires was commonplace. Nowadays it's mostly a rarity. And confusion now reigns supreme in the world of tires. You don't just go out and buy a set of tires anymore. No siree, buster. You consult with a tire expert, who grills you severely about your driving habits. Do you travel on highways mostly or a combination of highway and off-road? Do you pull a trailer? Do you have a good credit rating? (Well, that question might not necessarily be on the list, but can be applicable.)

In our area, winter weather was always severe. In the fall time, people usually switched over to winter tires.

That was when rear-wheel drive was the only game in town. So you likely had one set of two tires set aside specifically for winter driving. They had big mean looking deep lugs and sometimes sported little steel "studs". Even if all you owned was a big old sedan, you could go places with relative ease. In the springtime you generally replaced these rear tires with summer treads.

We're now overrun with all-season tires. But there are even variances between the all-season tires that cause deep-furrowed wrinkles to appear in the foreheads of otherwise normally patient drivers. Analyzing tread patterns tied in with associated warranties can cause one no end of grief. And a set of new tires can be a pretty big investment. You want to be reasonably certain you've purchased a good product.

The glut of four-wheel drive vehicles in the market today has pretty much assured that large, deep-lugged, white-lettered absolutely mean looking tires will grace many tire retail storefronts. Never mind that most of the vehicles sporting these "climb-every-mountain-with-ease" tires will likely never leave city limits. I'm always astounded how so many people can even afford these vehicles, never mind the huge, fancy tires.

And now many major chain stores are selling their own brand of tires. But you know they have to be made by one of the major tire manufacturers. Don't they? Some of the tires have some pretty creative names suggesting such and such tread would be ideal for your application. Being a macho fellow, one certainly wants to get the meanest sounding name. After all if you own a four-wheel drive and see a tire description that reads with "arides-soft-like-a-marshmallow" versus "one-tough-aggressive-go-anywhere-you-rough-looking-stinker" it's pretty much a no-brainer. Even if you only go grocery shopping in the city.

I'm in the market for some tires. The tire experts I've consulted with have done their job adequately. I'm completely confused and once more yearn for simpler times. Our vehicle falls into the light-truck category. There are approximately 211 possibilities in tire selection among the massive number of tire brands out there that would supposedly be suitable for our vehicle. Tire brochures should feature a toll-free help line ---- to address the intense inner struggle that ensues within the fragile male ego thereby possibly adversely affecting ones personal relationships, whilst pursuing the ultimate tire for their vehicle. Or something like that.

# The Bedtime Snack

The healthy eating advocates would be having forty fits if they saw my bedtime routine. A few soda crackers topped by a few chunks of ridiculously old cheddar cheese chased by a cup of tea make up my 9:30 PM ritual. Otherwise I won't sleep. So medically, it's a toss-up. And my Dad's to blame. Therefore I win this round.

It seems that when we were younger and well past the teething stage (generally performed on a venison bone) I graduated to crackers and cheese for my evening snack. Dad usually did this, so it was quite natural that I too adopt the practice. He too enjoyed the old cheese. The stuff that was virtually on the edge of extinction was deemed really good. Which meant that if the cheese was held up for inspection to the Aladdin lamp, a slight greenish hue was present. On the cheese.

There are some drawbacks to eating this cheese. The major drawback occurs when you add a slice of onion and perhaps a sardine to the mix. A couple of these snacks and you can stun a fly into total submission during mid-flight simply by blowing gently in its general direction. The combination is potent, but the sleep benefits far outweigh the breath aesthetics.

Popcorn is also a great little snack. On the farm we had one of those screened gizmos with the long handle. You shook it gently over the stove plate area until two things occurred. One is that the popcorn would pop to the extent the screen was bowed on top. The other thing actually signified that each tiny-popcorn was indeed popped. The popped corn would either smoulder and emit threads of smoke or erupt into flames. That's when you put it into the bowl and added salt and butter.

We've now got one of those electric air-poppers. It's pretty darned convenient. Throw in a scoop of popcorn, place a bowl underneath and walk away. You can tell when it's done simply by the fact it quits popping and whirls away undisturbed. Once you've cleaned up all the popcorn that overflowed the bowl when you forgot to turn it, you're pretty much ready for the salt and margarine - yes, margarine. Thank you for the sympathy. I agree. It is a sad state of affairs these days when butter is considered a luxury. It's a darned good thing our old cows aren't around to see what I slather on my toast now. In fact come to think of it, I'm not even sure what I actually slather on my toast. Only that it's called margarine.

It's funny how some rituals from childhood or at least until leaving home remains so ingrained in ones adult life. I've always liked tea. Not the herbal tea. Just plain old tea without any sugar or cream. Again Dad drank that, so I did too. In harvest time, he got his delivered out to the field in a quart sealer with a sock around it for insulation. And garden fresh cucumber sandwiches made with real homemade bread baked in a woodstove. Slathered with real churned butter. I used to go along just to sit down and partake of this feast. A simple snack, but I can still vividly taste it today in my memory.

I've never gotten used to eating cookies before bedtime. Or cake. For some obscure reason that doesn't show up anywhere in Monty's Bedtime-Snack Food Guide. Which is very weird since oatmeal or peanut butter cookies are likely to be chosen over fine caviar by yours truly.

Dear-at-Heart picked up a small package of bologna the other day. That used to be a household staple back in my younger days. In fact it was actually much more then a household staple. Even after leaving home I'd make bologna sandwiches on a regular basis. Then it was outlawed due to the lack of good taste and surprisingly, also higher cost. But that bologna the other day tasted darned good. Now I'm yearning for more bologna. With soda crackers, old cheddar cheese and onion. Plus a cup of tea. Now that's a bedtime snack.

# Meetings & Numb Butt

"Sorry sir, but Mr. Dolittle is in meetings for the remainder of this year. Perhaps if you call back during the first week of next year, you'll catch him at his desk. He generally sets aside the first week of any given year to plan that coming year's meetings." "Pardon me?" "Oh no sir, I have absolutely no idea who would look after doing that work. We haven't actually done any work here for a number of years now. We just meet and discuss stuff." "What's that?" "Mmmm, yes, I agree, it must be a sign of the times."

Now the above conversation might be a tad exaggerated, but not much. It's incredible how many meetings take place these days. And it seemingly occurs at all levels of any given organization. Bureaucracy reigns supreme.

Many people really do only attend meetings today. They discuss theoretical wishes and call them objectives. Or goals. In case someone in the real world questions them on their duties, they'll loftily reply that they're working on a vision-statement.

Meetings are in vogue today. For a very short while, your importance was apparently gauged by mobile phones. Hence there was a market for fake mobile or cellular phone aerials to mount on your vehicle. That fad faded. Now you're "tied up in meetings". And your self-worth immediately escalates up a notch or two.

But what do you tell your kids? How do you pass on all that "working-life" knowledge that your dad gave to you? Here are a few suggestions.

"Make certain you take a briefcase into your meetings. It doesn't matter what's in it, just take one with you."

"Look interested and have a piece of paper in front of you. Here are a few games you can play using only a pen and paper that'll keep you occupied for a couple of hours."

"Practice sitting for long periods of time on hard wooden chairs. Eventually you'll find that your fidgeting will be reduced. It's called numb-butt training."

"Never, ever doze off. If you get sleepy, pinch your ear and bite your tongue. If your sleepy spell becomes unbearable, fake a massive coughing fit. If it's a really good one, everyone will stop their own doodling and refill their water glasses too."

What's even more remarkable is that today we've got communication devices that can do virtually anything. You can be "live-chatting" with someone thousands of miles away via your computer. Both of you can see and hear each other. Nah, that's only for personal chitchats.

Another moniker in today's corporate world is to "do-lunch". Its popularity has rapidly spilled over into everyday life. The "doing-lunch" crowd runs rampant. In hindsight I guess we used to "do-lunch" too. At noon we'd all sit down together, open our tin lunch buckets and chow down on whatever sandwiches were in there.

It's sobering though to think that thousands of people upon reflecting on their life's accomplishments, and if honest, will only say "I met". And their large callused still numb-butt will be proof positive.

# My Dented Head

Fortunately I still have some semblance of hair on my head. It masks the dents, scars and other unsightly blemishes associated with a half-century old beat-up head.

When man was created and the first one rolled off the assembly line, it was likely with the thought that his bony head structure would simply be there to protect his brain. Basically a toolbox. As an afterthought a couple of eyes were added, then a nose, two ears and a mouth. I have heard on good authority that the first model had only one eye in front, with another at the back. Unfortunately man was in a continual state of confusion over whether he was actually going backward or forward. The redesigned and current model ended up with two eyes in front.

Woman also received two eyes in front, but the other eye in the back was inadvertently left in place. Woman, being self-conscious of her image, grew long hair to keep this third eye hidden. But that eye could still see. This small design oversight has wreaked havoc on mischievous youngsters (and most adult males) for centuries. Isn't it amazing what you can learn nowadays?

From day one my head was the first thing to get damaged in the line of duty. And having your eyes built right into your toolbox doesn't help matters. If you want to see anything your head has to lead the way. But your eyeballs must operate on slow transmission lines.

Let's take an open cupboard door. Your eyeballs know it's there. Heck they helped you open it. But inevitably you smuck it anyway. Your ears heard the thump; your nose smelled the burnt hair during the scrape and your mouth even put in its two cents worth with a small "eek". Shortly after all this damage has occurred your brain receives a weak signal from your right eyeball saying there's an open cupboard door at two o'clock high.

In today's world both eyeballs would have likely been designed such that you could pull one out on its data cable, peer into say, the engine compartment and then allow it to naturally retract back into its socket. My head once ended up stuck firmly between the engine block and the firewall. My ears never fully recovered from that incident. While my head was in reverse the ear support re-bar must have gotten warped. Both ears were pasted to my skull for an extended period of time in that ultra painful forward/downward position also known all too well by those who try to put on a tight fitting motorcycle helmet.

Man has tried natural means of protecting his skull. In the 50's and 60's great gobs of grease provided a sticky barrier able to withstand all but the most severe head whacks. In the 70's man allowed his hair to grow long. Large curly hairdos became popular. It looked like a sheep was perched on some heads. But alas, now my hair is disappearing. And the toolbox is in pretty rough shape. Caulking and spray paint?

## Birds without Feathers

He swaggered into the party and immediately attempted to dominate all conversation. With his swollen head bobbing to and fro, it took only moments for one and all to label him the "turkey". It's actually quite fascinating to compare birds with people. The traits are remarkably similar.

Crows are loud and obnoxious. They wake you on mornings when you're desperately trying to get a few more moments of shuteye. They can sense when some hapless camper is suffering from a severe hangover. Perched immediately above the hangoveree's tent, these obviously intelligent birds will cut loose with "caws" of immense intensity. The sound is designed to grate on alcohol-saturated nerve endings like fingernails on chalkboards.

The hangover- laden person will at first mumble a muffled "go-away". This quickly escalates to screams of "get-out-of-here-you-blank-bitty-bop-bag-of-feathers". It finally culminates in a half-dressed, bleary-eyed, foul-mannered excuse for a human being emerging in a rage from his tent to throw a smelly shoe at the intelligent crow. The crow laughs hysterically and heads off to his next victim. We all know people like that.

Great blue herons are majestic birds. They stalk proudly about with occasional swivels of their head and from this great height look down disdainfully on the small world beneath their feet. If hungry, they'll likely just stab a small fish. In the back. For as far as they're concerned, there's lots of small fish in the world beneath their feet. Doesn't that sound familiar?

Hummingbirds are flighty little things. Constantly moving about in their quest for food. They never have a weight problem, because of their high metabolism. They're hard workers, quite sociable and very entertaining. They never overstay their welcome and in fact we don't even like to see them leave. They're admired greatly and people instinctively want to help them.

Birds of prey or raptors are fierce looking. They're intense and hardly ever break that look or show any visible emotion. Feared and respected, but perhaps a little bit lonely? Or maybe they prefer it that way? Outside of immediate family, they pretty much keep to themselves. Up close, they appear to look through you, not at you. A visit can be a tad uncomfortable.

Magpies are pretty birds. Noisy birds though and particularly so when in the company of other magpies. They're not overly well liked, but appear to be quite intelligent. Incredibly perceptive, they can almost sense your intentions and will flit off even when you're quite certain they haven't even seen you. They prefer socializing only with other magpies. But they are pretty and you're quite apt to hear that comment from people who see these birds for the first time. Beauty is truly in the eyes of the beholder.

The gull family is mostly associated with garbage dumps and farm machinery working in fields. Some of these birds can be quite large and seem to have an admirable ability to eat anything and come out smiling.

They're also cheeky. While traveling by ferry, one gull intentionally dropped a small stone on our vehicle. Overly bold, they'll practically steal a sandwich right out of your hands. They thrive on discarded stuff, but will also gobble up young birds and eggs with equal enthusiasm. This doesn't do much for their image and in most cases they're tolerated, but certainly not liked.

Then we have the songbirds. Lovely to look at, lovely to hear and their vocalization automatically puts people in a good mood. People put out attractants just so a songbird or two will take up residence in their yard. Everyone likes the songbird and dislikes the neighbourhood cat that likes songbirds for an entirely different reason. Songbirds make good neighbours. Too bad there weren't more songbirds.

So there we go. What types of birds do you know? One bird wasn't included. Although relatively rare, we do see the odd turkey vulture. Now that's scary.

# A Disposable Society

This news was too amazing for me to even comprehend. Self-destructing discs specifically geared toward those movie rentals that you generally forget to return on time anyway. Now to begin with we thought the transition from Beta to VHS format was a mammoth technological swing. But now it appears most everyone is moving toward DVD's. And supposedly somewhere in the not too distance future there will be no need to return these DVD's on time. At a pre-selected time the content will go "poof" and the James Bond feature nestled in your humble abode will be kaput.

We're living in a truly disposable society. It's getting downright scary. Garbage disposal is supposedly a major concern and efforts to encourage recycling are of paramount importance. But then we see the likes of handy-dandy food storage containers that you just turf out after use. Ditto with the latest ads on those disposable "cutting" boards. And that's only a tiny sampling.

Disposable razors have been around forever. Disposable baby diapers as well. It's the new stuff coming on the market that dazzles me. For some reason we seem to be on that old course of double standards. On the one hand, use items that are recyclable. On the other hand, here use this, it's nice and handy and can be thrown in the garbage after one use.

A personal peeve for me is certain coffee shop retailers offering the chance to win gift items that are printed on the disposable coffee cup. So you go into the store with your travel mug, fill it with coffee and then you're also given an empty disposable cup to check out for a prize. The nearby garbage is now chock-full of these perfectly fine, but now defective, disposable cups. To me, that's a blatant waste.

This "disposable-mania" seems to have spilled over into all aspects of society. Mechanics of old used to fix certain parts on vehicles. Now those same parts are just replaced. Maybe it's a trade-off given the per hour costs these shops now operate under. Another thing that puzzles me about vehicles today is their relative lack of unreliability. We have space stations in place and almost weekly space flights, but in 80 some years, we still have a zillion things that can and do go wrong with brand new vehicles.

Way back in my early days when $150.00 could still buy a decrepit, but drivable (the definition of drivable being rather loose) vehicle, these were sometimes deemed disposable. However the majority of them were recyclable given the fact they generally ended up in a junkyard for parts. Most were an environmental and road-safety menace of great proportions.

The engines on these treasures were likely worn out to the extent liquefied exhaust was expelled on a continuous basis in the form of used oil. You simply couldn't afford to buy new oil and have it going straight through the engine and out the pipe at an alarming rate. So in a sense we were recycling back then. So long as the used oil from the local garage never had any solid objects present, it was usually deemed perfectly fine. When the car finally wheezed its last and passed out on some stretch of road, you "disposed" of it and promptly bought another environmental disaster.

Husbands have always been disposable. Apparently the market is currently overloaded with these used hubbies. On the plus side, most are recyclable and generally environmentally friendly. You're most apt too see them wandering about at singles dances or sitting in bars looking forlorn. They wear wrinkled shirts and appear unshaven. No one looks after them anymore. But with a little rejuvenation, most are likely good for several more years of wedded bliss with someone. A word of caution is in order though. Some of these wrinkly fellows might be confirmed bachelors and quite enjoy their own company. Best leave those fellows alone.

So where will we stop with disposable stuff? I suspect more and more of our everyday items will continue to come on the market in the form of disposable or throw away. Combine that with our rapid growing technology sector and we might have an entire society of disposable human look-alikes. Wow, I could feasibly throw myself out someday - that's a sobering thought.

# Keeping Our Dogs Entertained

Fact one. Dogs are incredibly intelligent animals. Fact two. People do really stupid things. Fact three. Dogs notice. Fact four. People think, thank goodness no one saw that. Fact five. The dog did and he thinks you're really stupid.

I've nearly always had a dog in my life. We have loads of dog pictures. And the dogs were pretty much all smiling in those photos.

Most dogs are predictable. They have a good disposition and outside of being fed and watered, simply want to enjoy life. With wagging tails, laughing eyes and joyous barks they're undeniable people pleasers. People though are notoriously unpredictable. Severe mood swings are a given. Outside sources can have a major impact on your mood. It has to be confusing to a dog.

You might be wrestling and clowning around with Rover when your significant other arrives home bearing mail. You pause in your playing, open an envelope and immediately turn into this ultra-grumpy person. Rover's stumped. He wonders what the heck that's all about? He still wants to play, but decides the fact you've thumped the table and uttered really weird sounds means playtime has ended.

Rover sees you at your worst. You're getting ready to leave for work. It's Monday morning. No one likes a Monday. You probably had too much garlic in the lasagne last night as your mouth has an absolute horrid taste. You have an all-day meeting to attend. You're certain these are an absolute waste of time. You're in a foul mood. Grouchy even. Rover thinks maybe he'll lie over by the door and be a casual observer. Especially when you spilled the "gotta-go" coffee on your clean white shirt. And there goes those weird sounds again.

If Rover accompanies you to the garage, he's in for a real treat. You go out the door whistling, fondly boxing Rover's ears and saying really goofy things. He's in his glory. You enter the garage and look forward to doing the oil change on the old clunker. Rover lies by the garage door. Partway out. Dogs are intelligent animals. Rover knows there's going to be a change in attitude within a reasonably short period of time. Dogs are perceptive.

But you're still whistling. Hey, the oil change is going great. You've just added the third litre when you notice an oil puddle seeping out from under the tire. It hits you like the head-plop from a mile high seagull. You forgot to replace the oil plug. Immediately following a bellow of "great gol-dings, two dah-dahs and a big gosh" you kick the tire. Rover thinks to himself, now that might hurt. You leap about on one leg clutching your incredibly sore foot and making more of those weird sounds. Rover thinks he'll go and lie under the tree.

That night as Rover is stretched out by the fireplace, you notice him kicking and yelping in his sleep. "Likely chasing rabbits", you chuckle knowingly. Well, Rover is indeed dreaming. But in it he's laughing hysterically at his master's entertaining antics.

Ain't Life Grand!

# Outdoorsy Direction Skills

I've always fancied myself to be reasonably outdoorsy. It started shortly after birth, probably a by-product of having been teethed on a venison rib bone. But one isn't just born outdoorsy. You have to acquire a knack for it. And determining your direction relative to not only north, south, east and west but where such and such is located is key to being outdoorsy savvy.

Misconceptions due to ample quantities of ill advice distributed from highly incompetent outdoorsy wannabes are a common problem for youngsters. I have good reason to believe this contributed greatly to my initial low outdoorsy self-esteem. But thanks to good books and sound advisement from truly outdoor savvy individuals, I've since learned much. A lot of my learning though was from trial and error.

Telling someone that there's a really good gopher patch located directly under the large white fluffy cloud that bears a remarkable resemblance to an upside-down apple pie gives you limited credibility. Apparently clouds do tend to move about with some rapidity. It took several hours to find the young friends that I'd generously let in on my secret gopher patch. Thank goodness there was a relatively calm west wind that day.

The revelation that clouds are subject to winds which obviously also occur way up there was sobering. So I resorted to placement relative to livestock and other target points. For instance, I'd tell my friends to line up the large post with the magpie on top with the brown cow that had a crooked tail. Look immediately below that on this side of the fence for the huge badger hole. About twenty feet east of the badger hole and directly in line with the patch of lady-slipper flowers is a funny looking rock. There's a garter snake sunning itself by that rock. This method had flaws. My credibility was fast being eroded.

One of my books said old time trappers and scouts relied upon astute observation and awareness of their surroundings at all times. This became my motto. I excelled at wildlife observation and would dazzle my young peers by identifying birds or animals at exceedingly long distances. Not only that, but I'd quickly give them the numbers of birds in a flock or animals in a herd. There were some initial minor stumbling blocks. But I caught on to these eventually. For instance there's really no advantage to counting the number of legs in a herd of deer and then dividing by four to determine the exact number of deer. What if one of them only had three legs? It happens. Nature can be cruel.

Much of my learning had to evolve through trial and error. Recovery time for maintaining credibility was sometimes dependant upon a quick comeback. For instance the time one of my young peers said he'd heard there were other ducks besides mallards and teals. I said oh yeah, but you can't really call those slough ducks "ducks". Further investigation within my books revealed there were indeed all kinds of ducks with all kinds of names. In fact there were way too many types of ducks for me to even remember. Let alone identify. So I eventually settled on my own version of scientific identification - mallards and those other ducks.

Compass and map reading was and still is unbelievably complicated. Initially I thought the north arrow on a compass pointed north and that was that. If I wanted to go south I'd just follow the other end. East and west was at right angles or in between north and south. How foolish of me. Someone said that little arrow didn't really point true north. Being outdoorsy and of obvious high moral character, the last thing I needed was a lying compass. So I resorted to using the hands on my watch and the sun's position. Then I got a digital watch for a present. I'm still honing my outdoorsy skills.

## Signs of Confusion

Highway directional signs at interchanges and off-ramps can be terribly confusing. Others may be quite clear even to drivers totally unfamiliar with the area. For some reason it must be a no-no for a design team to repeat the same general interchange configuration too often. They're likely severely chastised at performance appraisal time. They must be allowed one practical interchange design followed by four intensely confusing ones in any given year. That's my theory anyway.

You'll be merrily motoring along highway 27778223 anticipating finally arriving at your son's new home. It's somewhere over there, generally speaking. Just off highway 27778223A. Your map says the turnoff is not too far ahead. Your map would lead you to believe it's a piece of cake to gently swing onto highway 27778223A. Your map is a liar.

There are 4 lanes of traffic and all the drivers are fulfilling a childhood fantasy to race with each other at breakneck speed. You're trying to look for a sign showing the turnoff ramp and still maintain some semblance of vehicle control. Forget about the speedometer. The last time you glanced at it while sandwiched on four sides between a Mack truck, a Hummer, a big Dodge 4 by 4 and a 1962 Volkswagen van (that was worth a second look) you were clocking out at 140 kph. Your sign says you need to be 2 lanes over and quite quickly.

Turn signals are meant to show your intentions and thereby avoid accidents. Road ethics would dictate that fellow drivers show some courtesy and allow you to graciously move over into the desired lane. Activating a turn signal on highway 27778223 is like dropping the start flag at a drag race. The entire herd speeds up one more notch taking you with them. The ancient hippie in the Volkswagen van is looking quite serene and surrounded by a halo of questionable smoke. The bald guy in the Hummer is chewing his big cigar and giving you his very best glare complete with a Hollywood patented squint. He's in the right-hand lane that you need to be in. You're now doing 150 kph.

If you slow down the big Mack will quite simply run over you. This was made clear when you attempted to slow down slightly and in your rear view mirror now saw only a large slab of chrome. The hippie might be vulnerable. You ease over his way and offer him a pleading look. He shows some compassion and slows down. You quickly veer into his lane and launch forward into a new pack. It's exhilarating. This is great. You're now dodging in and out of traffic oblivious to the honking horns and one-fingered salutes. Oblivious to your turn-off onto highway 27778223A.

A service station several kilometres down the road has a payphone. And bathrooms. They only show stick figures to differentiate between ladies and gents rooms. It must be a no-no for these bathroom door designers to follow the same guidelines across the country. That's my theory anyway.

A Good Lunch Spot - Lost?

# Monty's Favourite Bannock

Premix 2 cups flour, ½ tsp. salt, 2 tsp. baking powder, 1 tbsp. sugar and ¼ c. powdered milk. (Multiply ratio as needed.) Scoop 2 cups of mix into bowl; add 1 c. cold water a little at a time, while kneading. (Raisins & fruit optional.) Spread dough evenly in a well-oiled pan. Cook slowly until browned. Oil top; flip over. (Easy to say!) Check for stickiness in center. None? Slice, split, butter, jam and enjoy! (May also be cooked on a stick over a fire.)

Cooking bannock on sticks -
a picture taken many moons ago!

## Dear-at-Heart's Kokanee Chowder

Dice up one farmer's type coil sausage and fry lightly until cooked c/w one large onion (make sure onion is nicely browned).
Cover w/3 to 4 cups of water in a stockpot or like-sized larger pot.
3 potatoes (cube or cut into hashbrown sized pieces) – place into pot.
Add:
1 tsp. garlic pepper
3 rounded tsps. bacon bits
1 level tsp. steak spice (Montreal Steak Spice © or similar)
½ tsp. oregano
1 tsp. seasoning salt
Cook until potatoes are done.
Clean 3 to 4 scaled Kokanee (depending on size, wash well, remove head, tail & fins)
Put into soup pot (on top of potatoes, sausage, onions), simmer for 4 minutes one side, flip, simmer 4 minutes other side, take out & remove bones, put boneless fish pieces (desired size) back into soup (may add shrimp, crab or other seafood if available).
Add 3 cups 1% milk, ½ cup cream (canned milk or similar), 2 tbps. margarine or butter, stir into soup until just dissolved (nearly to a boil) , season with additional salt if desired.

Mmmm - right off the camp stove!

# Basic Preparation for Kokanee Chowder

Onion & Potato preparation

Farmer's Sausage frying

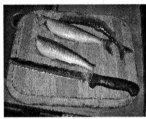

Preparing the Kokanee

Simmer 4 minutes per side

Looking for a great gift idea? Or would you like to purchase additional copies of this book or any of our other books?

Check your local bookstore or you can order directly from us:

"A Bit of Bulltufis!"         "What if Cows Yodeled"
(ISBN 0-9689800-2-3)         (ISBN 0-9689800-1-5)

"Tales 'n Such from a Dodge City (Saskatchewan) Boomer"
(ISBN 0-9689800-0-7)

Name: _____

PO or Street Address: _____

City or Town: _____

Province: _____

Postal Code: _____

Note: If this is to be a gift, please specify the details c/w mailing address and a signed copy of the chosen book(s) will be sent on your behalf directly to that person. E-mail queries to: rvmonty@shaw.ca

Cost is $19.00 Cnd. for each book (includes postage, handling and GST).

Please forward and make your cheque or money order payable to:

Ron Montgomery
PO Box 133
Crowsnest Pass, AB T0K 1C0